Pâté, Confit, Rillette

Pâté, Confit, Rillette

RECIPES FROM THE CRAFT OF CHARCUTERIE

BRIAN POLCYN with MICHAEL RUHLMAN

W. W. NORTON & COMPANY
Independent Publishers Since 1923
New York   London

For information about permission to reproduce selections from this book, write to
Permissions, W. W. Norton & Company, Inc., 500 Fifth Avenue, New York, NY 10110

For information about special discounts for bulk purchases, please contact W. W. Norton
Special Sales at specialsales@wwnorton.com or 800-233-4830

Manufacturing by Asia Pacific
Book design by Toni Tajima
Production manager: Anna Oler

Library of Congress Cataloging-in-Publication Data

Names: Polcyn, Brian, author. | Ruhlman, Michael, 1963– author.
Title: Pâté, confit, rillette : recipes from the craft of charcuterie / Brian Polcyn
with Michael Ruhlman.
Description: First edition. | New York : W. W. Norton & Company Independent Publishers since 1923,
[2019] | Includes index.
Identifiers: LCCN 2018049773 | ISBN 9780393634310 (hardcover)
Subjects: LCSH: Pâtés (Cooking) | Cooking (Foie gras) | Cooking (Pork) | LCGFT: Cookbooks.
Classification: LCC TX749 .P63 2019 | DDC 641.6/64—dc23
LC record available at https://lccn.loc.gov/2018049773

W. W. Norton & Company, Inc., 500 Fifth Avenue, New York, N.Y. 10110
www.wwnorton.com

W. W. Norton & Company Ltd., 15 Carlisle Street, London W1D 3BS

1 2 3 4 5 6 7 8 9 0

For Julia and Ann

CONTENTS

PART 2

Mousse ↓ 99

Contents

Contents

Contents

FOREWORD
by Jacques Pépin

Pâté, Confit, Rillette: Recipes from the Craft of Charcuterie is an essential, much-needed book about a branch of gastronomy that has been amazingly neglected in America until recently, even by the best-known culinary schools.

From the old French word *chaircuitier*, or "cooked flesh," the word charcuterie refers to cooked dishes, mostly from pork offals and usually lowly scraps of meat. It also refers to the place where these products are sold, *à charcuterie*, and to the name of the craftsman, *charcutier*, who specializes in the making of these dishes. So the making of ham, sausages, pâtés, tripes, pigs' feet, kidneys, blood sausages, sweetbreads, saucissons, hot dogs, and many more dishes that have been well respected and admired forever in Italy, France, Spain, Germany, and even China, are finally becoming part of the American cook's curriculum.

I remember that when I was a child in Lyon, the charcuterie stores were more important to the cooks than butcher, fish, or vegetable stores. The charcutiers were the original caterers, where fish, quenelles, whole fish in aspic, several pâtés, cooked roasts, various salads—from snout to potato—meat pies, mousses, rillettes, and even stuffed artichokes were all offered, as well as cheeses and vegetable gratins, like chard, cardoon and potato.

For me, the humble country pâté is still the perfect first course in a holiday meal. The charcutiers are craftsmen with very specific recipes and procedures. Although I rarely follow a recipe in my cooking, in charcuterie making, I do. Proportion, seasoning, cooking time, and temperature are essential ingredients of the recipes. Often, the making of special terrines, ham, saucisson, and blood sausages are left to the professional, but it is fun, easy, and rewarding for the home cook to make good pâté, head cheese, tripe, rillette, or breaded pigs' feet. Prepared with modest, ordinary ingredients, charcuterie is the art of the miserly cook and a good pâté is usually determined by the proportion of meat to fat, the proper seasonings, and the cooking temperature and process. Finally, in *Pâté, Confit, Rillette*, this branch of the culinary arts is getting the recognition it deserves. I can't wait to cook from it.

INTRODUCTION

A beautifully made pâté is a wonder—and not only for the pleasure of eating it. A great pâté is a representation of the heights of culinary craftsmanship and excellence. Yet this simple mixture of meat, fat, salt, and spices is also a preparation born of economy and thriftiness, a way to put scraps to use, a method likely thousands of years old.

But that is what true cooking is all about: taking scraps and, with knowledge and care, transforming them into delicious nourishment, both noble and humble, that is a delight to behold and a pleasure to eat, nourishing on every level.

Yet the pâté is not always thus.

Since we first published our book *Charcuterie: The Craft of Salting, Smoking, and Curing*, a book that contains a chapter on the *pâté en terrine*, we have eaten countless pâtés. At home in suburban Detroit, Brian teaches the craft to students. And he travels the country teaching the craft to chefs, always making pâté after breaking down a whole hog to make use of the abundant trim and fat. We have gone to restaurants where chefs send us charcuterie boards with their own creations. We have traveled to Paris and to Lyon, France, to taste the work of Gilles Vérot, perhaps the finest maker of pâté in that country, even the world. And we have driven an hour south of Lyon, to the small town of Tain-l'Hermitage, to attend the pâté world championship. In short, over the course of more than a decade, we've eaten all manner of pâté.

And they're not all the wonder described above. They are often dry. Or they crumble on the palate, a textural disaster. Or they have no flavor. At many American restaurants, where the chef is otherwise accomplished, we've been served mediocre pâté. Even in France, the world's pâté epicenter, we have eaten ho-hum pâté. Some recent books on the subject offer photos of overcooked terrines and shoddy technique and recipes that don't work.

Why? Because pâté can be made well or it can be made poorly. The cook can choose excellent ingredients or cheap ingredients. The cook has the knowledge of what makes a pâté great or the cook does not.

Brian likens the situation to the liver and onions his grandmother cooked and the liver and onions he learned to prepare under a master chef. His grandmother used liver that had been frozen. She cut it unevenly and cooked it to death even as she undercooked the onions. But with renowned Michigan chef Milos Cihelka, Brian learned how to prepare fresh calf's liver, carefully removing the veins and slicing it ½ inch/1 centimeter thick, which makes it very easy to cook to medium-rare. He dusts pieces with flour, then sautés them in hot oil till they're nicely browned but still rare. He then splashes brandy into the pan, flames it, and removes the liver. Next he sautés the onions until they are lightly caramelized, then returns the liver to the pan, warms the slices with the onions, and brings them to medium-rare. That is a delicious way to prepare liver and onions.

All these small steps build upon each other for the final result. Bad decisions likewise build toward the opposite effect.

No cooking is particularly difficult. It's simply a matter of knowing what the steps are and paying attention as you work your way through them. This is especially true of pâtés, and the reason for writing this book: We love pâtés and hoped to explore how to perfect them, how to make them great.

Over the past decade, interest in charcuterie in this country has exploded. *Charcuterie* is a broad term for all those preparations that were created in order to extend and preserve meat—whether taking raw scraps of meat and offal and creating a pâté en terrine, grinding and stuffing sausage, or curing a ham. Charcuterie boards in restaurants have become commonplace. Chefs across the country are dry-curing their own *saucisson*; some restaurants, such as Portland's Olympic Provisions, even created a separate business out of it.

Our book was a factor in this resurgence, but the main reason for it, we believe, is that once American chefs and cooks discovered the centuries-old practice of charcuterie, they found its virtues so clear that they embraced it on a national scale. This is not a fad— these techniques have been around for centuries. In America, they're here to stay and will continue to evolve as America creates its own charcuterie traditions in our ongoing culinary evolution. Our goal in writing *Pâté, Confit, Rillette* is to continue to elevate this ancient and sublime craft, to make it accessible to as many people as possible, and to feed those who hunger for more.

Pâtés are a form of charcuterie (the word comes from the Middle French *chair* for "flesh" and *cuite* for "cooked"). Confit, meat poached in fat so that it will remain preserved in that fat for one, two, or three years, is another branch of the craft. And rillettes are a kind of combination of the two. Of all charcuterie preparations, pâtés, confits, and rillettes are perhaps the most accessible to the home cook, and ones that, with care, can be elevated by chefs and ambitious home cooks to extraordinary levels of elegance. They represent the most authentic, honorable, and exciting form of cooking we have: transforming lowly scraps into the ethereal, which is the cook's highest calling and most thrilling achievement.

WHAT EXACTLY IS PÂTÉ?
(And a few other definitions)

Back when we wrote *Charcuterie*, many people asked if pâté was a liver spread, or just assumed that there was liver in whatever the stuff was—they weren't sure. This is possibly because the main pâté Americans had been offered for decades was pâté de foie gras—pâté made from the happily fattened livers of ducks and geese. That or some form of chicken liver spread, what we would now call chicken liver mousse or a refined version of the great Jewish classic, chopped liver. These are indeed some of our favorite pâtés. Some people love the deep, iron-y flavor of liver, and others do not. Most appreciate the depth of flavor a judicious amount of liver, ground with the meat, gives to a finished pâté.

But it need not contain liver in order to be pâté. Pâté, literally "paste" in French, is ground meat and fat, cooked. That's all. Sometimes it's referred to as *pâté en terrine*, which simply means that the pâté is cooked in a terrine mold—similarly, a vegetable terrine is a preparation in which vegetables are cooked or bound in a terrine mold.

Confit, a term that derives from the word *preserve*, is a form of preservation that originated with duck and geese. The method is simple: Salt the duck for a day, poach it in its own fat (so plentiful in these birds), and then store it in this fat. Properly prepared, the method will preserve the duck for years. While it has been used as a preservation technique for centuries, we continue to confit duck and geese and other meats nowadays simply because meat prepared this way is so delicious. Exhumed from its lardy slumber, a duck leg can be reheated in minutes in a hot oven or under the broiler to offer delectably crisp skin and impossibly tender, deeply flavored meat. Indeed, the term *confit* has such deep connotations of deliciousness, we now even refer to vegetables cooked in fat as a type of confit.

Rillettes are a cross between the pâté and the confit. The meat is cooked in the style of the confit or it is braised, but it's then shredded, enriched with fat and seasoned, and put in a mold. It's served more like a pâté, most often spread on a toasted baguette.

But the three preparations that give this book its title are all variations of meat and fat prepared in a way meant to make this meat last, and in doing so give us some of the best food possible.

We should note a few other definitions: **Pâté en croûte** means literally "pâté in crust," or pâté cooked in dough. Usually such preparations are made in some sort of mold, but freeform pâtés en croûte are possible—though we would usually refer to them as meat pies.

You may hear the term **forcemeat**, or **farce**, often used in the charcutier's kitchen (and used interchangeably throughout this book). They mean simply ground meat. It's an ugly word, the anglicized version of the lovely French word *farcir*, meaning "to stuff." It began, apparently, as *farce meat*, meat that is to be used as a stuffing (ground meat that is to be pumped into casings, for instance), and evolved into *forcemeat*.

Mousse is a puree of cooked food, often enriched with cream, with a soft, smooth texture, as in a chicken liver mousse. In its sibling preparation, the **mousseline**, raw food is pureed, usually with cream, and is then cooked. A shrimp mousseline, for example, is a puree of raw shrimp, cream, and egg white; this can then be put into a mold, with lots of fresh herbs and lobster and scallops, then cooked to make a shellfish terrine. **Quenelles** are dumpling-shaped portions of mousseline, typically formed using two spoons, then dropped into stock or water. This is a good strategy if you're working with very bony fish, which is one reason pike quenelles are a staple in French bistros.

Interior garnish is the term we use to describe any item that is mixed into the ground meat—nuts, whole chunks of meat, herbs—to provide visual contrast to the ground meat, a tantalizing mosaic, in addition to flavor. And **structured inlay** is the rather formal-sounding name for any large piece of meat, or any ingredient, that is placed in the center of a terrine, such as a whole pork tenderloin. (See page 32 for specific information on garnishes.)

We often make special forms of pâté. The **galantine** is typically a poultry pâté that is rolled in the skin of the bird, poached, and cooled in stock, then served cold. In this book we prepare a similar seafood galantine—rolled, cooked, chilled, and served cold. The **ballotine** is the same thing, only it is roasted and served hot.

Gelée is the term we use for any liquid that sets to a sliceable gel at room temperature, whether from the natural gelatin in meat stock or from powdered gelatin. This is also referred to as **aspic**.

FOR CRYING OUT LOUD, WHY BOTHER?

One last word about the pâté en terrine, separate from rillettes and confits: care. The latter are no-brainers and take no more effort than, say, making beef stew or a Bolognese sauce. If you're not a committed home cook but want the benefits of delicious charcuterie preparations, stick to those recipes in this book. Pâtés, on the other hand, require effort and, especially, care.

So, honestly, why bother? Well, you're still reading, so that's one reason: You're curious. Making a pâté requires multiple steps and at least one, often two, countertop appliances (a grinder and a standing mixer). It requires careful attention once it goes in the oven. It requires at least one full day before you can eat what you've made. And generally, you have to pay attention to *all* the steps or you may compromise the terrine you've put so much effort into (though it should be noted that even mistakes and carelessly made pâtés are edible—and usually pretty delicious).

If we cook in a restaurant, we make pâtés for the reasons restaurants have always made pâtés: They're practical. When Brian was an apprentice, he asked his mentor, Chef Milos, why do we make these? His chef said, "It tastes great, it utilizes byproducts, it's got a low food cost, it keeps for a long time in the refrigerator, and it reminds me of my youth. Did I mention that it tastes great?"

Taste! It can all come down to that one word.

We bother also because we like to cook, and this is cooking at its highest level, and therefore gives the cook the greatest satisfaction. And there is no greater satisfaction than cooking hard and well for people who are important to you.

If you're having guests for dinner, this is a terrific way to make the day-of preparations easier, since you can make your pâté up to a week ahead. A slice of pâté with some whole-grain mustard and a small arugula or watercress salad on the side is an elegant, delicious, and inexpensive first course. And it makes great leftovers if you don't use the whole pâté.

We want to reiterate that this is not thirty-minute-meal cooking, so if you don't like cooking, or find cooking to be an unrelieved chore, we recommend you give this book to a friend who likes to cook, preferably one who loves to cook and who also invites you over all the time. You'll thank us.

And to all cooks who undertake the noble pâté in any of its forms, we bow to you.

PART 1

Pâté en Terrine

We begin with the glory and the raison d'être for this book: the pâté en terrine. In this chapter, we'll go over everything you need to make expert pâtés of all kinds. We'll address the tools you need, our Rules to Live By, the general principles of pâté making, and a rough description of the techniques and methods shared by all pâtés. Then we'll give master recipes for the four fundamental types of pâté forcemeats, or farces: gratin, straight, country, and mousseline.

THE TOOLS YOU WILL NEED

Generally speaking, rillettes and confits don't require any special tools, but pâtés do. Tools are important to any craft. And keeping your tools in good working order—that is, cleaning them and keeping all blades and dies sharp—is as important as using them properly.

Meat Grinder

The first tool you'll need for pâté is a grinder—it's how you turn chunks of meat and fat into paste. If you don't have one and don't want to get one, there are several pâté recipes that require only a food processor (see page 22). If you have a butcher whom you trust and who will follow your exact instructions, he or she should be happy to do the grinding as recommended in each recipe. Grinder attachments for standing mixers are available, but after using several of them, we can't recommend them; they're not sharp enough and the motors are not strong enough for a clean, distinct grind. (That said, if you have such an attachment, we'd rather you make a pâté than avoid it because of your grinder—so go ahead and use it; just be aware of this caveat.) A standalone grinder is ideal; they start at about $50. The stronger the motor, the better.

A word about the dies and blades:
Brian feels that the size of the dies is very important, so we are specific about the sizes. We recommend that chefs preparing these recipes hew to these sizes for the best results. That said, if your machine comes with die sizes different from the ones we specify, use your common sense when following the recipes.

Remember that these blades become dull and need sharpening, so we advise finding a sharpening service near you that can sharpen both blades and dies. Sharp blades for grinding the meat are one of the most important factors in successful pâtés, so we can't stress enough the importance of starting with sharp blades, caring for them after you've used them (washing and drying by hand, storing them securely so they don't rattle around in a drawer and dull), and sharpening them regularly. This issue is so important to Brian that he has one blade devoted to each die he uses, a practice and expense he recommends to any chef wanting to excel at this craft.

Standing Mixer

This is one of the most valuable appliances in the kitchen. It's a big-ticket item that's worth the expense if you cook (and certainly if you bake). In this book, and in the craft of charcuterie generally, we mainly use the paddle attachment to mix country pâtés and rillettes. Mixing has two important functions: to distribute seasonings and garnish evenly and to develop the protein myosin in the meat, which helps bind the pâté. This is best accomplished with a standing mixer, but it can, theoretically, be achieved using a stiff wooden spoon and a lot of elbow grease.

Food Processor

Most kitchens have these, and they are essential for mousselines and straight and gratin pâtés. In the days of Escoffier, fish was pounded by hand and then pressed through a drum sieve to achieve a smooth mousseline. Happily, we no longer have to do this. Today there is really no alternative method to the food processor for those recipes that call for one.

Again, the sharpness of these blades is fundamental to the success of the puree. If you're still using the processor you got as a wedding gift fifteen years ago, it's worth buying a new blade for it before making pâtés that require a processor. As with the blades and dies for his grinders, Brian keeps one blade specifically for pureeing meats for pâtés, and another blade for all other food processing.

Tamis/Fine-Mesh Sieve

Some recipes call for the puree to be passed through a sieve, or tamis, to achieve a refined texture. Any fine-mesh sieve will suffice to catch any of the longer strands or connective tissue that haven't been fully pureed.

Terrine Molds

These are convenient but not absolutely essential. You can, after all, make a pâté by rolling it in plastic wrap to form a log, wrap this tightly in foil, and then poach it. But molds are cool to look at and to serve from, and they have many uses, so we think they are worth the expense. They come in all manner of shapes and sizes. We use the industry standard, Le Creuset's 1½-quart/1.5-liter lidded terrine mold. Most of the pâté recipes in this book are scaled to fill this size terrine. These terrines will yield approximately 15 appetizer-size portions.

Pâté en Croûte Molds

Molds made specifically for the purpose of cooking pâté in a crust have hinges that allow you to take the mold apart in order to remove the pâté without damaging the crust. It is not essential for making pâté in a crust (after all, meat pies are a form of pâté en croûte), but it is a fundamental piece of equipment for the classic preparation. They're considerably less expensive than terrine molds.

Thermometer

An instant-read thermometer of some kind is essential for knowing when your pâté is done. The most convenient kind is a cable thermometer, which has a probe that remains in the food throughout the cooking, attached to a countertop monitor. A digital instant-read is the next-best choice.

Roasting Pan

Pâtés require the gentle heat of a water bath, so you'll need a roasting pan large enough to hold your terrine mold.

Knives

All cooking—everything you need to do in a kitchen—can be done using two knives, a chef's knife and a paring knife. No one needs a block with twelve knives. It's a good idea to invest in quality with these two fundamental knives. A boning knife with a thin, semiflexible blade is good to

have as well but not mandatory. The only mandatory requirement where knives are concerned is sharpness. Keep your knives as sharp as lightning. We recommend using a professional wet-grind service if there is one in your area.

A slicing knife is preferable for cutting terrines, but it is not mandatory; if you don't have one, use the thinnest blade you have.

RULES TO LIVE BY

All crafts follow specific principles, and the craft of charcuterie is no different. Pay attention to them, follow them, and your pâtés will be excellent. Ignore them and they won't be. It's as simple as that. What follows are our rules to live by when making pâtés.

Temperature

Temperature is one of the most critical factors when making pâtés or any kind of forcemeat that requires the uniform blending of meat and fat—temperature of the ingredients, temperature of the tools, and temperature of the air. Cold is essential for keeping fat bound to protein, and this is one area where the home kitchen can have an advantage over the restaurant kitchen. Restaurant kitchens are often very hot, and keeping ingredients below 40°F/4°C is harder there than in cooler home kitchens (unless it's August and you don't have AC). So if you're making pâtés and sausages in a restaurant, find the coolest part of the kitchen at the coolest time of the day. Always remember, the colder the better. Ideally all ingredients are just above freezing when you're grinding, pureeing, and mixing them.

Time

This kind of cooking takes time, so give yourself plenty of it. Few things make cooking more difficult and un-fun than when you're rushing. When you rush, you tend to take shortcuts. Shortcuts compromise the pâté. There are no shortcuts here, or in any excellent cooking.

Proper Equipment

Use the right tools for the job and keep those tools in good shape. In the case of pâté, this primarily means having a good grinder and good food processor, both with very sharp blades.

Ingredients

That you use quality ingredients should be a given. There's a reason for the restaurant adage "Garbage in, garbage out." It's hard to make mediocre ingredients into excellent dishes. In charcuterie, try to use meat raised by a grower who cares about that meat rather than the industrial meat at your grocery store. When using liver, try to get the best-quality liver you can find—again, ideally from local farmers.

It's best if you're able to use meat that hasn't been frozen. The uniform blending of fat and protein in a pâté is an emulsion, fat suspended in a network of water and protein. Water is important in creating and maintaining the emulsion. When frozen meat thaws, it loses water.

A few of these recipes call for pink curing salt. This product, salt with sodium nitrite, goes by various names: DQ Curing Salt #1, Insta Cure #1, Prague Powder #1, and TCM (tinted cure mix). They are all the same. Pink curing salt prevents spoilage from harmful microbes and creates the distinctive piquant flavors of bacon, corned beef, and other preserved meats. In these recipes, it's used exclusively for color and so is optional.

Seasoning

There are two kinds of seasoning: salt and everything else.

Salt is critical to flavor, so you want to be sure to use the right amount. And remember that food eaten cold requires more salt (about 2 percent by weight) than food eaten hot (usually 1 percent by weight, but often more depending on what you're making).

Like most chefs I've worked with, Brian uses Diamond Crystal kosher salt, which has no anticaking agents. But it is much lighter than the other common kosher salt, Morton's, which is what I use. I'm simply used to how much I pinch when I season. Our general recommendation is to always use the same salt so that you get used to seasoning by hand. I find it difficult to season meat with Diamond Crystal because I have to add twice as much by sight as I think I should because it's so light; I invariably end up undersalting my food.

Sea salt is, of course, fine to use, but again, depending how finely it's ground, it will have a different weight relative to its volume than kosher salt.

The most important point when using salt for the recipes in this book, then, is to always weigh your salt for accuracy. If you're not using a scale, we recommend that you use Morton's kosher salt to measure by volume.

Other seasonings, primarily spices, should be fresh. Ground spices that have been sitting in a spice rack for longer than you can remember are going to have a different effect than spices that are fresh. As a rule, it's best to toast spices whole—30 seconds in a hot, dry pan should do it—and grind them as you need them. We offer two pâté spice blend recipes that go with different meats (see pages 33 and 34).

Cooking

Most of the cooking here is done in the gentle heat of a water bath, which we'll discuss in "The Basic Steps for All Pâtés" (page 27).

When searing food—in the gratin preparations, for instance—we use high heat. Allow your pan to get very hot before adding the oil, and once you've added the oil, allow the oil to heat before you put the meat in. The meat you add to this hot pan should be as dry as possible, since moisture will cool the oil. When you lay the cold meat in the hot oil, don't touch it until it's well seared—often cooks are afraid that the meat will stick, so they move it around in the pan immediately, which is exactly when it *is* stuck; it effectively unsticks itself from the pan as it sears. These are all fundamental principles of sautéing generally, but because searing is so important for flavor in pâtés, which will be eaten cold, it's especially worth noting here.

Fat Separation: Troubleshooting

Since most forcemeats are between 40 and 50 percent fat, it's important that the fat not separate out of your mix during cooking. Fat separation, a broken emulsion, is the number one reason a pâté fails. Generally, there are five reasons fat might separate out of forcemeat:

1. The number one reason fat separates out is heat. To prevent this, it's critical that everything stay very cold. The meat and fat should never be left to sit out at room temperature. Before grinding and pureeing the meat and fat, it's best if they are on the verge of freezing, stiff with cold. If you're slow in butchering it, keep whatever you're not working on in the freezer until you're ready for it.

2. Another form of heat we tend not to think about is friction. The friction of grinding the meat heats it, as does the friction of pureeing the meat in a food processor. This is why we recommend that you grind meat into a metal bowl that's set in an ice bath; ideally you will also have chilled the bowl in the freezer first.

3. The cutting blade in the grinder or food processor is dull.

4. The farce is cooked at too high a temperature. Foods that are high in fat require low and slow cooking, which is why we always cook our pâtés in a water bath in a 300°F/150°C oven, below boiling temperatures.

5. Too much liquid is added. Reductions play a key role in flavoring pâtés, but the reduction should be of syrup consistency so you have all the flavor without the diluting qualities.

A WORD ABOUT MEAT GENERALLY AND ABOUT THE PIG SPECIFICALLY

It should go without saying that the quality of meat varies depending on how that particular animal was raised. The most inexpensive pork found at the most inexpensive grocery stores is commodity pork; it will have very little flavor and be unnaturally lean. We are aware that everyone's budget differs, but we do recommend buying from stores that source their meat conscientiously or, better, from the growers themselves if this is available to you. If there is a Whole Foods Market near you, these stores tend to have excellent meat. Medium-size independent grocers are often good sources of meat. And of course growers' markets can not only offer the best quality, they can often get you the odd bits unavailable at stores (a whole pig's head, for instance, or pork back fat).

I use the pig as the example because its meat and fat are the anchor of this culinary specialty. Its creamy, neutral-flavored fat is perfect for enriching pâtés and rillettes. Its meat offers uncommonly diverse flavors. Beef runs tough to tender, lean to well marbled, but it all tastes pretty much the same: beefy. Lamb is basically lamb. Chicken has light meat, which is very mild, and dark meat, which is more flavorful. But pork seems to have a whole range of flavors and textures depending on where on the animal it comes from. The quality of the animal's raising is immediately apparent in the color and flavor of the meat and the quality of the fat. You can create preparations of astonishing diversity from a single animal, more than from any creature on earth. Pork can be silky prosciutto, succulent baby back ribs, soppressata, bacon, tender pork chops, crunchy cracklings, crispy pig ears, or a country liver pâté.

The pig is nothing short of a miracle creature offering extraordinary bounty.

The common cuts of the pig used here are primarily the shoulder (also known as the butt), the belly, and the layer of fat that runs along the back of the animal, sometimes referred to as fatback but more accurately called back fat.

The shoulder is a heavily worked muscle and so needs to be tenderized either through cooking or through cutting and grinding. It is also one that is well marbled and therefore very flavorful and succulent. This makes it the perfect meat for making sausage (see our book *Charcuterie*) or sausage's close cousin, pâté.

The pig has fat of varying consistencies. Some fat is squishy; other fat is firm. And leaf lard, which is the fat from the viscera surrounding the kidneys, is, when rendered, especially dense-white and creamy and is especially prized for bakers of savory pastries. If you can get your hands on it, we urge you to try using it to make any of the doughs in part 4, "Crust."

Back fat is more common and easily acquired. This is the fat that runs over the loins, which run down either side of the tall spine (when you see a pork chop with a layer of fat around the loin part, that's part of the back fat). You may need to special-order it from wherever you buy your meat.

If you can't find back fat, using fat from lower down on the pig, the belly, is acceptable. Keep in mind that depending on where on the belly it comes from, it might be half fat and half meat. The fat becomes softer the closer it gets to the back leg; that mushy fat is not the best for pâté. The belly is a great cut because of its abundant fat and, like the shoulder, is a heavily worked and therefore flavorful cut.

THE BASIC STEPS FOR ALL PÂTÉS

What follows are the basic steps to follow for making all pâtés—and the reasons for them. Flip back to these pages for reference when preparing any of the pâté recipes in this book.

Cutting Meat to the Right Size

This should be common sense, but it needs to be emphasized: All meat that is to be ground should be diced or cut into strips small enough that they don't need to be forced down the feed tube of the grinder. The less your grinder has to work, the better your grind will be. After you've cut the meat, it should be returned to the fridge and completely chilled or put on a baking sheet in the freezer before being ground.

The Ice Bath

Because we want to keep the meat as cold as possible all the time, and because grinding heats the meat through friction, we grind our meat into a metal bowl set in an ice bath. An ice bath is simply a larger bowl filled with about 60 percent ice and 40 percent cold water; the goal is for ice or ice water to be in contact with the entire surface of the metal bowl that is set in it, where the ground meat will soon be.

Grinding and Pureeing

Grinding determines the texture of the finished pâté. Pâtés can be coarsely or finely ground. For the most part we like them all fairly well ground, even country pâté, so grinding is a critical step for two reasons. First, grinding helps develop the myosin protein in the meat, which is sticky and creates a good bind. Second, the grind

is an important factor in creating a stable meat-and-fat emulsion, a mixture in which the fat is uniformly distributed (as it is in baloney or mortadella, or in a hotdog or other finely textured sausage). The bind and the emulsion are the primary factors in a pâté's texture, its luxuriousness.

We use four different sizes of dies for grinding: ⅛ inch/3 millimeters, ¼ inch/ 6 millimeters, ⅜ inch/9 millimeters, and ½ inch/12 millimeters. The dies typically have some sort of indication on them of their size, such as "1-4" for ¼ inch, or "6mm" for 6 millimeters. (You can always measure the hole with a ruler if there's no indication on the die itself.) We will always specify which die is optimal. We know that not everyone has the same dies, and some may simply have one large die and one fine die (these are usually ⅜ inch/9 millimeters and ⅛ inch/3 millimeters). Use your common sense in determining which die to use. If a recipe calls for grinding through a ½-inch/12-millimeter die and you don't have one, use the one you have that is closest to that size.

Straight forcemeat pâtés and gratin forcemeat pâtés require a progressive grind, which, in most cases, means grinding the meat first through a ¼-inch/6-millimeter die (or ⅜-inch/ 9-millimeter die if that's what you have), then regrinding through a ⅛-inch/ 3-millimeter die. This results in a very fine texture and stable emulsion. (If you have a very powerful grinder, as Brian does—he uses a 3-horsepower Hobart, the Ferrari of grinders—you don't necessarily need to use a progressive grind.)

Some straight and gratin forcemeats may call for only a single grind through a large die. This is fine for a coarsely textured pâté, but one grind typically doesn't develop the myosin well enough to hold the pâté together. So to make up for the lack of binding, egg is added (the white is primarily protein), a tactic popularized by France's uber-charcutier, Gilles Vérot.

For country pâtés, we like a coarse grind; to ensure that it has a good bind, we regrind about a third of the meat through a fine die.

For mousseline forcemeats, the meat may not be ground at all, only pureed in a food processor. This is the case for chicken and seafood. Veal shoulder or duck thighs, though, may require grinding through a fine die before being finished in a food processor.

Grinding and Temperature

As always, temperature is the main force to be reckoned with when grinding meat for pâté, since the friction of grinding raises the temperature of the meat. The feed tube and grinder should be stored in the freezer until you're ready to use them. Once you've rechilled your meat and fat after dicing it, set your metal bowl in an ice bath. Then set up your grinder.

If a recipe calls for grinding the meat twice, store the first grind in the fridge (or in the freezer—just be careful not to let it freeze solid) while you change the die on the grinder and rechill it (at this point it may be quickest to chill the grinder in a bowl or bucket of ice water, but you can refreeze it).

If the pâté must be both ground and pureed in a food processor—or if you're making a mousseline, which requires only a food processor—store the bowl and blade of the food processor in the freezer until you're ready to use them.

Mixing

Country pâtés are mixed using a standing mixer fitted with the paddle attachment. Your meat should be very cold when you mix it, since you rechilled it in the fridge or freezer after grinding. We don't freeze the mixer bowl and paddle, but we do make sure that most additional ingredients (diced interior garnish, for example) are chilled.

The Quenelle Test

Before you cook your pâté, you will want to test it, mainly to check for seasoning (if it doesn't have a good bind or if the fat is separating out of it, there's not a lot you can do to remedy it). The most definitive way to do this is to roll a small cylinder of the pâté, the size of your thumb, in plastic wrap and poach it gently until it's cooked through, then taste it. If you want to be absolutely sure of the seasoning, chill it quickly in an ice bath, then taste—and remember, cold food needs to be seasoned more aggressively than food eaten hot. If you must expedite matters, you can sauté a small patty of it and taste, keeping in mind that you won't have the flavors from browning, and that it should taste slightly oversalted when eaten warm.

If the pâté is lacking in flavor or seasoning, add more salt or spice and remix until the seasoning is incorporated.

Filling the Pâté en Terrine

Line your terrine mold with plastic wrap to facilitate unmolding it. Cooking in plastic wrap is considered safe provided the wrap doesn't have plasticizers or the chemical BPA—which most brand-name plastic wraps do not contain. (If you remain concerned about the effects of cooking food in plastic, even at these low temperatures, line your terrine mold the old-fashioned way: with thinly sliced bacon or back fat.) Sprinkling water in the terrine mold helps the plastic wrap stick into all the corners. Use enough plastic wrap so that you have plenty of overhang to fold over the top of your terrine after the mold has been filled.

When the terrine mold has been filled with the pâté and you have pressed down on it with a rubber spatula to make sure there are no air pockets, fold the plastic wrap over the top of the terrine mold. Cover the terrine with a lid or with aluminum foil.

The Water Bath

All pâtés en terrine are cooked in a water bath. We'll give the instructions here to avoid making each recipe cumbersome with steps that are the same no matter what recipe you're making.

We use a water bath to maintain a low heat around the terrine mold, lower than boiling. Evaporation has a cooling effect and prevents the water from boiling in a 300°F/150°C oven (if you covered the pan, the water would boil).

Moving a big roasting pan filled with near-boiling hot water can be difficult, so we try to minimize this effort. At least 45 minutes before you want to cook your pâté, preheat your oven to 300°F/150°C. Place your empty terrine mold in a roasting pan and fill the roasting pan with hot tap water until it comes up to the lip or edge of the terrine mold. Remove the mold from the roasting pan. Put the pan in the oven so that the water will preheat along with the oven.

We use a combination of spatula and tongs to place the terrine in the water and to remove it. A large offset spatula is best to support the weight of the terrine, along with strong metal tongs to grip the edges of the mold. You may find it easier, when removing the terrine, to pull out the oven rack and remove the terrine mold from the roasting pan, then leave the roasting pan on the rack and allow the water to cool.

When you remove the cooked pâté, simply set it on your stovetop until it's comfortable to touch.

Pâtés not being cooked in a terrine mold are typically poached in water kept at 170°F/76°C. The only pâté not cooked in water is the ballotine, which is roasted and served hot.

Temperatures

For the best flavor, texture, and juiciness, we recommend cooking your pâtés to the following final internal temperatures, keeping in mind that they will continue to cook after coming out of the water bath.

> Foie gras: 118°F/48°C
>
> Duck pâté: 135°F/57°C
>
> Seafood pâté: 135°F/57°C
>
> Pork pâté: 145°F/63°C
>
> Chicken pâté: 160°F/71°C

Please note that these temperatures do not align with the USDA's food safety recommendations, which call for higher temperatures. We don't believe that those temperatures result in the best flavor. When the food is handled correctly and taken to our recommended temperatures, the dishes are both delicious and safe, but if you have concerns, please cook the pâtés to whatever temperature suits you.

Weighting and Cooling

As a pâté cools, it contracts. To help give it a uniform texture and shape as it does so, it's best to put a weight on top.

Cut a cardboard rectangle or thin piece of wood or plexiglass to the dimensions of the interior top of your terrine mold. Wrap this in aluminum foil. Once the terrine is out of the water bath and is cool enough to handle, put the terrine in the refrigerator. Place the rectangular board on top and place two or three canned goods on top of this (about 2 pounds/1 kilogram total).

Pâtés not cooked in a terrine mold, but rather rolled in plastic wrap and poached, should be removed from the poaching medium and transferred to an ice bath until thoroughly chilled, an hour or so. Pâtés such as a galantine, which is wrapped in cheesecloth and poached in stock, should be cooled as well (preferably in chilled stock).

It's important to allow the terrine to chill completely before unmolding—so while a pâté en terrine may seem fully chilled after 6 to 8 hours in the fridge, it's best to let it chill for at least 12 hours, or overnight.

Unmolding, Slicing, and Serving

Brian and I basically met over a pâté slicing table, when Brian was presenting his pork pâté to the judges of the Certified Master Chef exam as I was writing about it. There Brian had the entire setup for professional slicing and serving: the pâté, the sauce, plates, the *bain marie* insert filled with hot water, a slicing knife in that hot water, latex gloves, towels. Happily we don't always have to go through such efforts, though the setup is instructive.

To unmold a pâté from its terrine once it's fully chilled, remove the weight on top, then tug at the edges of the plastic wrap to loosen it. Upend the mold onto a cutting board; the pâté should come right out. If you are working with a delicate mousseline or if you are using fat or bacon as your lining, it's a good idea to set the entire terrine mold in hot water for a minute to loosen the pâté. Then simply unwrap your terrine and discard the plastic wrap.

To slice the terrine, hold the blade of your knife (if you don't have a slicing knife, use the thinnest, longest knife you own) under hot water, dry it quickly with a towel, and slice across the width of the pâté in one complete stroke forward. Heat the knife again under hot water, dry it, and do the same to make slices about ½ inch/ 1 centimeter thick.

Individual slices may be plated with a sauce of some sort—mustard or a chutney— and perhaps some greens, or slices may be served on a board with good bread and mustard on the side.

BINDERS

We use five main binders to strengthen the meat-fat emulsion and give the forcemeat an elegant texture, which is essential to the overall flavor and richness. They can also lighten a pâté.

THE ALL-MEAT METHOD. This technique relies on the meat's own protein, myosin, as the sole binder. The highest-quality meat, preferably meat that has never been frozen, should be used. It should be lean and trimmed of all connective tissue and fat. For the fat, pure, firm pork back fat is recommended, as opposed to random trimmed fat. Temperature is especially important when there is no added binder of the kinds described below, so be sure to

PÂTE À CHOUX PANADE

Despite our harping on working with everything super cold, this binder should be used at room temperature. If it's too cold, it can become lumpy in the pâté.

½ cup/120 milliliters whole milk

2 tablespoons unsalted butter

1 teaspoon/5 grams kosher salt

½ teaspoon freshly ground black pepper

½ cup/60 grams all-purpose flour

2 large eggs

1. In a thick-bottomed saucepan, bring the milk, butter, salt, and pepper to a boil over high heat. Add the flour all at once and stir quickly and continuously with a wooden spoon or stiff rubber spatula until the flour has absorbed the liquid and become a paste that pulls away from the sides of the pan—about a minute, if that.

2. Remove the pan from the heat. Allow the mixture to cool for a minute or two. Add one egg and stir quickly and vigorously until the egg is incorporated. When it is, add the second egg and do the same. (You can also use a standing mixer with a paddle attachment to incorporate the eggs; this is convenient when making larger batches but not worth the cleaning effort for this small amount.)

3. Transfer to a suitable container and cool to room temperature (or refrigerate for up to a day, then allow to return to room temperature before using).

YIELD: 8 OUNCES/225 GRAMS, ENOUGH FOR ONE STANDARD PÂTÉ EN TERRINE THAT CALLS FOR PANADE

keep all meats, fat, and equipment cold, cold, cold—but not frozen solid.

EGGS AND EGG WHITES. The egg white is composed of several different proteins, all of which help bind the pâté and improve its texture. Eggs have a neutral flavor, but from a functional standpoint, they are very powerful. Often only egg whites are called for (as in a seafood mousseline); when whole eggs are used, the yolk both enriches and lightens the finished pâté. The pork fat content can be lowered if you're using egg, though we never encourage lower fat on moral and flavor grounds.

BREAD. Moist, crustless bread is an excellent binder and lightener of forcemeats and one of the easiest binders to use. Any good-quality plain white bread, baguette, or country loaf is good. It's best not to use a heavy sourdough-style bread or other highly flavored bread. Soaking the bread in milk or heavy cream, and especially in beaten eggs, will create excellent binding and lightness.

PÂTE À CHOUX. Pâte à choux is one of the most versatile preparations, one that ought to be more prevalent in the home kitchen. It gives us cheese puffs and cream puffs (when baked), pasta-like dumplings (when boiled), and churros (when fried in oil). Milk (or water), flour, eggs, and butter—that's it. What's interesting is that flour is added to boiling liquid and cooked till it forms a paste, then eggs are stirred in. It's a fabulous binder in pâté as well, worth the small trouble of making (see the recipe above). This binder works especially well with lighter tender meats like poultry and fish but also with vegetables and pork pâtés. If too much pâte à choux is used, the end product may have a gummy consistency.

COOKED WHITE RICE OR POTATOES. Rice has a nice way of lightening up a pâté and giving it delicacy. Like bread and eggs, it is flavor-neutral and helps create a smooth texture. This binder works especially well with fish and vegetables. This is also a way to use a binder but keep a pâté completely gluten-free should you be serving anyone with celiac disease or severe gluten intolerance. Cooked potatoes are sometimes used for pâtés using light meats, such as veal, which is also a gluten-free binding option. But use a light hand, as too much of either can result in a gummy or sticky consistency.

GARNISHES

Garnish plays an important role in most pâtés, regardless of the type. Garnish adds color, a visually pleasing mosaic, varying textures, and, most important, flavor. How should you think about garnish in a pâté? As you would with any garnish for any dish: Does the taste contrast or enhance that of the pâté? Does it add the appropriate color? Is it the proper size? In a fine forcemeat, the garnish should usually be smaller and neatly cut. In a more coarse country pâté, the garnish may be unevenly sized and rough. Should it be random, small nuts or chunks of whole meat simply paddled into the pâté to wind up where they may? Or would the pâté benefit from a more structured approach, where you determine exactly where the garnish will stay in the finished pâté—a whole duck breast in a duck pâté, for instance? (This is referred to as a structured inlay and is completely enclosed in the pâté itself.) And

how much to use? Not more than half of the pâté, or you may weaken the structure of the pâté. But not so sparingly that it appears to be an afterthought.

What follows are a few suggestions for garnishes that work well with specific meat, fish, and vegetable terrines.

Pork

All confits (see pages 159 to 179) add a chewy texture and rich salty flavor to pork pâté. Smoked ham, smoked tongue, cooked sweetbreads, peeled pistachios or hazelnuts, pine nuts, cooked mushrooms, truffles, and some dried fruits (such as tart cherries, apricots, and prunes) all work to provide textural, visual, and flavor contrasts.

Game

Game benefits from the same garnishes pork does, especially the dried fruits—tart cherries, apricots, raisins, and prunes.

Poultry

In addition to the garnishes listed for pork, cooked hard vegetables also work for poultry, such as carrots or green beans. Roasted bell peppers are excellent. Soft leafy greens such as spinach or arugula also go nicely with neutral-tasting chicken. Soft herbs, such as tarragon or chives, which can be chopped or laid in as a whole structured garnish, are particularly flavorful.

Veal

Veal takes the same garnishes as pork with the exception of dried fruits, which do not work well with veal.

Fish and Shellfish

Soft leafy herbs, spinach, and cooked mushrooms are excellent in seafood pâtés, as are chunks of compatible-tasting seafood—whole shrimp in a lobster terrine, for instance.

Vegetable

Most vegetable terrines are light and soft like a custard. Any garnish, then, needs to be similarly soft and compatible so the pâté can be sliced cleanly—think cooked mushrooms, any of our vegetable confits (see pages 177 to 179), soft leaves of spinach or watercress, and soft herbs.

PÂTÉ SPICE BLENDS

Making your own fresh spice blend from whole spices that you toast and grind is one of the most influential steps toward making great pâtés. Even if you could buy commercial spice blends, as you can with pickling spices, your own spice blend would be so much better.

Brian's spice blends began with Escoffier and with his mentor, Chef Milos, back in the 1980s. Over the years he's developed combinations of spices that suit his tastes. You, too, should feel free to improvise, or follow his recipes, to the right and on page 34.

We recommend that you don't make more pâté spice than you will use over a couple of months, because the flavor will fade. Store unused spices in an airtight container in a cool, dark place or, better, in your freezer.

All-Purpose Spice Mix for Meat Pâtés

This is a great all-purpose blend. If you love the sweet spices, such as nutmeg and ginger, add more of those; if you like savory, up the herbs.

> 1 ounce/30 grams white peppercorns
>
> ½ ounce/14 grams sweet Hungarian paprika
>
> ½ ounce/14 grams ground bay leaves
>
> ¼ ounce/7 grams dried marjoram leaves
>
> ¼ ounce/7 grams dried thyme leaves
>
> ¼ ounce/7 grams ground nutmeg
>
> ¼ ounce/7 grams ground mace
>
> ¼ ounce/7 grams ground ginger
>
> ¼ ounce/7 grams ground cloves

1. Toast the peppercorns in a dry sauté pan. Transfer to a spice or coffee grinder.

2. Add the remaining ingredients and pulverize into a powder.

3. Store in an airtight container in a cool, dry place for up to 2 months.

Spice Mix for Wild Game

We don't include any recipes for wild game pâtés in this book, but many people who have access to game can use this blend, which is especially good for large furred game such as elk, deer, and moose, which have a stronger flavor.

½ ounce/14 grams white peppercorns

½ ounce/14 grams black peppercorns

1 ounce/30 grams juniper berries

½ ounce/14 grams ground mustard

¼ ounce/7 grams dried marjoram leaves

¼ ounce/7 grams dried thyme leaves

¼ ounce/7 grams ground bay leaves

¼ ounce/7 grams ground nutmeg

¼ ounce/7 grams ground mace

¼ ounce/7 grams ground ginger

1. Toast both peppercorns in a dry sauté pan. Transfer to a spice or coffee grinder.

2. Add the remaining ingredients and pulverize into a powder.

3. Store in an airtight container in a cool, dry place for up to 2 months.

Master Pâté Recipes

❖→⟩→❖→⟨←❖

The Gratin Pâté: Duck Pâté en Terrine

36

The Straight Forcemeat: Classic Pork Pâté

39

The Country Pâté:
Classic Pork and Liver Country Pâté

44

The Mousseline Forcemeat:
Chicken and Wild Mushroom Terrine

46

THE GRATIN PÂTÉ

In general culinary parlance, *gratin* means "browned." Thus, a gratin pâté denotes a pâté in which some or all of the meat has been browned or seared. We sear food to develop flavor. Almost all food tastes better when it has been browned in or under high heat. Because one of our biggest concerns with making pâtés is keeping ingredients very cold, it's especially important here to thoroughly chill your meat after it's been browned.

Duck Pâté en Terrine
(MASTER GRATIN PÂTÉ RECIPE)

If there's one recipe in this book that combines all you need to know about making a great pâté, this is it.

The first thing it requires is organization—of ingredients, equipment, and your time. You'll need to begin it the day before you intend to cook it because the meat needs to be marinated, and at least two days before you want to serve it, because you'll need to refrigerate it after cooking, with weights on top, until it's thoroughly chilled, typically overnight. This pâté involves searing, or browning, the meat (thus the term *gratin*). It calls for both random garnish and a structured inlay garnish. The standard grinding and mixing are involved, and, like most of the best pâtés, it has a high fat-to-lean ratio. All these facets and factors make this a fabulous terrine worthy of the effort.

This recipe calls for breaking down a whole duck, which gives you a lot more to work with (skin and abundant fat, the carcass for stock). But you can also make this with parts: 2 breast halves, which will weigh 4 to 5 ounces/110 to 140 grams each, and 12 ounces/340 grams leg meat.

1 (5-pound/ 2.25-kilogram) duck

1 tablespoon/ 15 grams kosher salt

2 teaspoons freshly ground black pepper

1½ teaspoons All-Purpose Spice Mix for Meat Pâtés (page 33)

¼ teaspoon pink curing salt, optional

½ cup/120 milliliters brandy

½ cup/120 milliliters Madeira wine

2 tablespoons minced garlic

2 tablespoons minced shallot

1 bay leaf

6 ounces/170 grams fresh duck livers, veins and connective tissue removed, separated into lobes

¼ cup/60 milliliters vegetable oil

6 ounces/170 grams pork shoulder, cut into 1-inch/2.5-centimeter dice

3 ounces/85 grams slab bacon, cut into 1-inch/2.5-centimeter dice

2 thick slices country bread, crusts removed (day-old bread is fine)

2 large eggs, whisked

12 ounces/340 grams pork back fat, cut into ½-inch/1-centimeter dice

½ cup/120 milliliters heavy cream, chilled

½ cup/45 grams shelled pistachios, blanched and peeled

½ cup/85 grams diced smoked ham or smoked tongue (¼-inch/ 6-millimeter dice)

¼ cup/30 grams black truffle peelings, optional

Day One

1. Remove both legs—drumstick and thigh—from the duck. Remove the skin from the breast, then remove both breast halves. Separate the tenderloins from the breasts. Remove any sinew from the breasts.

2. Remove the skin from the legs and reserve. Remove all the meat from the bones, then remove all sinew and tendons from the meat. You should have approximately 12 ounces/335 grams of leg meat and tenderloin. Season this meat with the kosher salt, pepper, spice mix, and pink salt (if using). Cover and refrigerate for at least 8 hours. (Reserve all the bones for stock.)

3. Combine the brandy, Madeira, garlic, shallot, and bay leaf in a bowl or plastic bag. Add the duck breasts and livers and toss to distribute the ingredients. Cover the bowl or seal the bag and refrigerate for at least 8 hours.

Day Two, Part One

1. Remove the duck breasts and livers from the marinade, leaving as much of the marinade ingredients in the container as possible, and pat dry. Discard the bay leaf and reserve the marinade.

2. Heat a sauté pan over medium-high heat and pour in enough oil to coat the bottom of the pan. Sear the breasts on both sides, browning them but leaving the centers raw. Transfer them to a plate. Add more oil if needed and sear the livers, leaving the centers raw. Transfer the livers to the plate with the breasts and refrigerate until they are thoroughly chilled, 20 minutes or more.

3. In the same pan, brown the pork shoulder and bacon on all sides. Transfer to a plate or bowl, cover, and refrigerate until thoroughly chilled.

4. Pour off any fat from the sauté pan, add the reserved marinade, and reduce over medium heat to a syrup consistency, being careful not to burn the residual sugars in the Madeira. Transfer the reduction to a small bowl, cover, and refrigerate.

Day Two, Part Two

1. Prepare a water bath in a 300°F/150°C oven (see page 29).

2. Put the bread in a small bowl and add the eggs.

3. Remove the reduction from the fridge and uncover so that it tempers (if it's too cold, it may not disperse completely).

4. Combine the chilled duck leg meat with the diced back fat and the seared pork shoulder and bacon. Grind through a ⅜-inch/9-millimeter die into a metal bowl set in an ice bath.

5. Add the bread-egg mixture to the ground meat mixture and regrind through a ⅛-inch/3-millimeter die into the bowl, still in its ice bath. This is a critical point: Take the temperature of the ground meat mixture using an instant-read thermometer. If it is too warm, above 45°F/7°C, spread out

RECIPE CONTINUES ↻

the meat on a baking sheet and put it in the freezer for 15 minutes, or until the temperature is below 45°F/7°C.

6. Transfer the ground meat to a chilled food processor bowl, add the wine reduction, and pulse until the meat mixture is completely smooth. Scrape it into a mixing bowl and, with a rubber spatula, fold in the cold cream.

7. Do a quenelle test (see page 28) and adjust the seasoning if necessary, remembering that cooked food served cold requires more seasoning.

8. Fold in the pistachios, ham or tongue, and truffle (if using).

9. Line a 1½-quart/1.5-liter terrine mold with plastic wrap and fill it one-third of the way with meat, making sure to press the farce well into the corners. Remove the duck breasts and livers from the fridge and pat them dry with paper towels. Lay the livers in a single layer, pressing them down into the farce. Fill the mold another one-third of the way with farce, smoothing it over the livers. Lay the breasts in a neat row on top of the farce with their thick ends toward either end of the mold and their tapering ends overlapping. Make sure they don't touch the sides to ensure that they will be completely enclosed within the farce. Fill the mold the rest of the way with the farce and fold the plastic wrap over the top.

10. Cover with a lid or aluminum foil and cook in the water bath to an internal temperature of 135°F/57°C, 45 to 60 minutes. Remove the terrine from the water bath. When it's cool enough to handle, weight the terrine (see page 30) and refrigerate until thoroughly chilled. Unmold, slice, and serve (see page 30).

YIELD: 15 APPETIZER PORTIONS

A PROPERLY STRUCTURED INLAY. THE FORCEMEAT COMES UP AND AROUND SO THAT NO PART OF THE DUCK BREAST TOUCHES THE TERRINE MOLD.

THE STRAIGHT FORCEMEAT

The straight forcemeat is exactly like the gratin forcemeat except that we don't sear or brown any of the meat. It's useful not just in its reiteration of the tenets of making beautiful pâtés, but for the basic forcemeat ratio, or formula—two of them actually—expressing a fat content of between 40 and 45 percent. By understanding the recipe as a ratio, we can work with any amount we happen to have on hand (see the sidebar on page 41). It's the most straightforward of the pâtés and the most utilitarian.

Classic Pork Pâté
(MASTER STRAIGHT FORCEMEAT RECIPE)

Brian created this pâté to show off not only the simplicity of the ratio but also the beauty of the straight forcemeat, and to reiterate the fundamental technique, which uses a double grind to ensure a great texture and stable emulsion. This recipe follows the first of the straight forcemeat ratios, equal parts meat and fat, half as much pork shoulder.

12 ounces/340 grams lean pork, cut into 1-inch/2.5-centimeter dice

12 ounces/340 grams pork back fat or skinless pork belly, cut into 1-inch/2.5-centimeter dice

6 ounces/170 grams pork shoulder, cut into 1-inch/2.5-centimeter dice

1 tablespoon/ 15 grams kosher salt

1 tablespoon freshly ground black pepper

2 teaspoons All-Purpose Spice Mix for Meat Pâtés (page 33)

1 tablespoon vegetable oil

2 tablespoons minced shallot

2 tablespoons minced garlic

1 cup/240 milliliters Madeira wine

2 large egg whites

½ cup/120 milliliters heavy cream, chilled

2 cups/480 milliliters appropriate garnish (see suggested garnishes, page 32)

1. Prepare a water bath in a 300°F/150°C oven (see page 29).

2. Combine the lean pork, back fat, and pork shoulder in a mixing bowl and add the salt, pepper, and spice mix. Combine well, cover, and refrigerate.

3. In a sauté pan with sloped sides, heat the oil over medium heat and sauté the shallot and garlic for a few minutes until soft, being careful not to brown them. Add the Madeira, turn the heat to high, and bring to a boil, reducing the wine to a syrupy consistency—you should have about 2 tablespoons. Watch this step carefully as you may have to adjust the heat up or down depending on the surface area of your pan, since Madeira has residual sugars that can burn. Using a rubber spatula, scrape the reduction onto a salad plate, set aside, and allow to reach room temperature.

RECIPE CONTINUES ➤

4. Grind the chilled lean pork, back fat, and pork shoulder through a ¼-inch/6-millimeter die into a metal bowl set in an ice bath. Regrind the meat through a ⅛-inch/3-millimeter die into the bowl, still in its ice bath.

5. Transfer the ground meats to a food processor, add the egg whites and wine reduction, and blend until smooth. This is a critical point: Take the temperature of the ground meat mixture using an instant-read thermometer. If it is too warm at this point, above 45°F/7°C, spread out the meat out on a baking sheet and put it in the freezer for 15 minutes, or until the temperature is below 45°F/7°C.

6. Transfer the pureed meat to a metal bowl set in an ice bath and fold in the cold cream with a rubber spatula.

7. Do a quenelle test (see page 28) and adjust the seasoning if necessary, remembering that cooked food served cold requires more seasoning.

8. Fold in the desired garnish.

9. Line a 1½-quart/1.5-liter terrine mold with plastic wrap and fill it with the pâté. Fold the plastic wrap over the top.

10. Cover with a lid or aluminum foil and cook in the water bath to an internal temperature of 145°F/63°C, 45 to 60 minutes. Remove the terrine from the water bath. When it's cool enough to handle, weight the terrine (see page 30) and refrigerate until thoroughly chilled. Unmold, slice, and serve (see page 30).

YIELD: 15 APPETIZER PORTIONS

STRAIGHT FORCEMEAT RATIO

Most standard preparations can be reduced to their fundamental proportions to create an all-purpose ratio by weight for that preparation. This is especially useful in restaurants, where you may have 20 ounces/560 grams of lean trimmed meat (say you have twenty duck tenderloins and other duck trim). You can't do a lot with that small amount, but combine it with fat and seasonings and you can turn that trim into twenty portions. This is an ancillary beauty of charcuterie in the restaurant kitchen: You find yourself with unusable trim, and with a bit of craft you can turn it into a starter course that you can charge $15 for; you've turned something that you might otherwise have discarded into $300. That's exactly what Brian would do at his restaurant—20 ounces of duck tenders would become "Duck Pâté with Pistachios and Michigan Tart Cherries on a Bed of Grilled Balsamic-Glazed Radicchio" or any number of iterations based on what he had on hand.

The first ratio, then, is 2 parts lean meat, 2 parts fat, and 1 part pork shoulder, plus 2 percent salt and, as needed, spices, aromatics in a reduction, egg white (for binding), and cream. Using this ratio for the aforementioned amount of lean meat, you would make this pâté:

20 ounces/560 grams lean duck

20 ounces/560 grams pork back fat

10 ounces/280 grams pork shoulder

2 tablespoons/30 grams kosher salt

Minced shallot as needed

Duck or chicken stock as needed

Madeira wine as needed

All-Purpose Spice Mix for Meat Pâtés (page 33) as needed

Heavy cream as needed

Random interior garnish, as desired (see page 32)

As long as you maintain the meat-to-fat ratio, stick to a good salt percentage (2 percent for items to be eaten cold), and follow the basic straight forcemeat method, you will have a fabulous pâté. If you have more pâté than you can fit in one mold or not enough to fill a mold, you can make a roulade: Wrap it up in plastic and poach it, so your vessels' sizes don't matter.

Another way of expressing the ratio is 100 percent lean meat, 100 percent pork fat, 50 percent pork shoulder. Using this ratio, if you had that same 20 ounces/560 grams lean meat, you would use the same weight of fat. You would next multiply the amount of meat by 50 percent to determine the amount of pork shoulder, 10 ounces/280 grams.

To calculate the amount of salt, you would add the weights of the meat and fat together to get 50 ounces/1400 grams, and multiply this by 2 percent, or 0.02, to get 1 ounce/28 grams (about 2 tablespoons).

The rest is up to you to put your knowledge and experience to work. What kind of aromatics do want (shallot, onion, fresh herbs) and what kind of reduction (stock, wine)? Do you want more fat? Fold in cream. Will it benefit from a panade (see page 31) or some other form of binder? By all means, incorporate this as well. And finally, choose some kind of interior garnish (see page 32). Then simply follow the method, which you've embraced with heart, head, and soul. This is when you're really cooking.

CHICKEN AND WILD MUSHROOM TERRINE
(MASTER MOUSSELINE FORCEMEAT RECIPE, PAGE 46)

CLASSIC PORK PÂTÉ
(MASTER STRAIGHT FORCEMEAT RECIPE, PAGE 39)

DUCK PÂTÉ EN TERRINE
(MASTER GRATIN PÂTÉ RECIPE, PAGE 36)

CLASSIC PORK AND LIVER COUNTRY PÂTÉ
(MASTER COUNTRY PÂTÉ RECIPE, PAGE 44)

THE COUNTRY PÂTÉ

The country pâté uses humble ingredients—pork shoulder and liver, onion, and garlic—coarsely ground. It's an unfussy but richly flavored pâté. Part of the meat is ground twice to develop enough myosin to ensure a good bind. If you want to keep it extremely humble, you can even choose to omit the interior garnish.

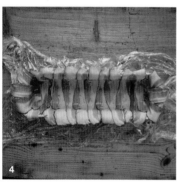
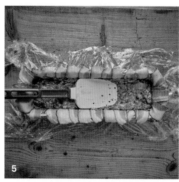
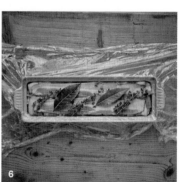

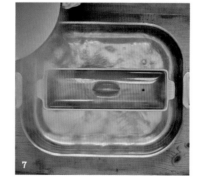
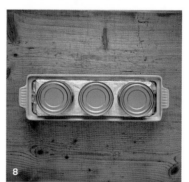

1: Two grinds, one coarse, one fine.

2: Combining all remaining ingredients.

3: Fully mixed country forcemeat.

4: Mold lined with bacon (see pages 28–29).

5: Filling the mold; be sure to pack the forcemeat into the corners.

6: Pâté fully encased in bacon with thyme and bay leaves for aromatics.

7: Terrine in the water bath.

8: It's important to press the terrine when it comes out of the oven, before it cools.

Classic Pork and Liver Country Pâté

(MASTER COUNTRY PÂTÉ RECIPE)

For the master recipe we offer the most classic of pâtés, with just enough liver to add a depth of flavor but not taste overly liver-y.

> 2 pounds/1 kilogram boneless pork shoulder, cut into 1-inch/2.5-centimeter dice
>
> 4 ounces/110 grams pork livers or chicken livers, veins and connective tissue removed, cut into 1-inch/2.5-centimeter dice
>
> ¼ cup roughly chopped onion
>
> 1½ tablespoons minced garlic
>
> ½ cup/48 grams coarsely chopped fresh flat-leaf parsley
>
> 2 tablespoons/30 grams kosher salt
>
> 1 teaspoon freshly ground black pepper
>
> ½ teaspoon All-Purpose Spice Mix for Meat Pâtés (page 33)
>
> 2 tablespoons all-purpose flour
>
> 2 large eggs
>
> ½ cup/120 milliliters heavy cream
>
> 2 tablespoons brandy
>
> 1 cup/240 milliliters garnish (diced smoked ham, confit, cooked mushrooms), optional

---

1. Prepare a water bath in a 300°F/150°C oven (see page 29).

2. Grind the pork through a ⅜-inch/9-millimeter die into the bowl of a standing mixer set in an ice bath.

3. Transfer about one-third of the ground meat to another bowl and add to it the livers, onion, garlic, parsley, salt, pepper, and spice mix. Grind this mixture through a ⅛-inch/3-millimeter die into the same mixing bowl with the remaining coarsely ground pork, still in its ice bath. Refrigerate or freeze until thoroughly chilled.

4. In a small bowl, combine the flour, eggs, cream, and brandy and stir to blend. Add this panade to the ground meat and seasonings. Add the garnish, if using.

5. Fit the bowl into the standing mixer and, using the paddle attachment, mix at medium-high speed until the panade, seasoned finely ground meat, and coarsely ground meat are uniformly mixed and the forcemeat become sticky, about a minute.

6. Do a quenelle test (see page 28) and adjust the seasoning if necessary, remembering that cooked food served cold requires more seasoning.

7. Line a 1½-quart/1.5-liter terrine mold with plastic wrap and fill it with the pâté. Fold the plastic wrap over the top.

8. Cover with a lid or aluminum foil and cook in the water bath to an internal temperature of 145°F/63°C, 45 to 60 minutes. Remove the terrine from the water bath. When it's cool enough to handle, weight the terrine (see page 30) and refrigerate until thoroughly chilled. Unmold, slice, and serve (see page 30).

YIELD: 15 APPETIZER PORTIONS

THE MOUSSELINE FORCEMEAT

This is probably the most versatile of all the forcemeats, as it can be put to such a great variety of uses. As ever, it's simple: pureed meat, cream, egg white, and seasoning. The term itself is not synonymous with *mousse* (see page 101). Mousseline forcemeat is a raw product—usually meat or fish—that is pureed, enriched with cream, and set by cooking, usually with added egg white or gelatin. It can be a pâté on its own; it can be a binder for other ingredients; it can be a component in a hot meal (quenelles in a soup, for instance); and it can be true to its farce nature as a stuffing (for raviolis, say).

The mousseline forcemeat is also a great one to make if you don't have, or don't want to use, a terrine mold. Instead, this pâté can be rolled in plastic wrap into a neat cylinder and poached. All pâtés can be made this way, in fact, but the mousseline forcemeat is especially suited to the roulade shape because it is so delicate.

MOUSSELINE FORCEMEAT RATIO

As with the straight forcemeat, the mousseline is especially useful because it offers such a versatile ratio. You can make a mousseline out of any white meat or seafood by following this formula, which comes straight out of Escoffier's 1903 culinary bible, *Le Guide Culinaire*: 1 pound/450 grams meat or seafood, 1 egg white, 1 cup/240 milliliters cream, plus salt and seasonings. The mousseline is the most delicate of the four basic forcemeats, but sometimes you will want more binding, and choose to use 2 egg whites instead of 1. Other times you will want a richer, softer mousseline, and add up to twice the cream. But the base ratio is a solid one, and the more mousselines you make, the better feel you'll have for how varying the ingredients affects the finished forcemeat.

For a mousseline, the meat is typically simply diced and pureed, though if you use a denser muscle—veal or pork, for instance—it's best to grind the meat before pureeing it, as with the straight forcemeat method.

In terms of adjusting the ratio to suit your purposes, determine what kind of result you want and how it will be used. Is it going to be a terrine served cold? If so, then less cream and more egg white will yield a firm but not rubbery sliceable product. Serving hot, as in quenelles? Then use more cream and less whites to yield a lighter, more delicate texture that is perfect as an elegant garnish for soup or as an appetizer—lobster quenelles with lobster Armagnac sauce and black truffles, for instance.

Here is the basic ratio—essentially 2 parts meat and 1 part cream bound by 1 egg white per pound/450 grams—and method for a mousseline forcemeat.

1 pound/450 grams white meat or seafood

1 or 2 large egg whites

Kosher salt as needed

Freshly ground black pepper as needed

All-Purpose Spice Mix for Meat Pâtés (page 33) as needed

Pinch nutmeg, optional

1 to 2 cups/240 to 480 milliliters heavy cream

1. Prepare a water bath in a 300°F/150°C oven (see page 29).

2. If the protein is soft, like chicken breast or shrimp, simply cut it in small pieces; firmer protein should be ground first. The meat should be as cold as possible, no higher than 40°F/4°C, without being frozen solid—it's best if it's stiff with cold. Combine the cold meat in the food processor with the egg white(s) and seasonings.

3. Puree the meat (depending what type it is, it may ball up around the blade). Scrape down the sides at least once to ensure even blending. With the motor running, add the cream in a slow but steady stream.

4. For a very fine, smooth texture, scrape the mousseline into a tamis or fine-mesh strainer. Press the mousseline through the tamis into a metal bowl set in an ice bath.

5. Do a quenelle test (see page 28) and adjust the seasonings if necessary, remembering that cooked food served cold requires more seasoning.

6. If adding garnish, fold it in now.

7. Line a 1½-quart/1.5-liter terrine mold with plastic wrap and fill it with the pâté. Fold the plastic wrap over the top.

8. Cover with a lid or aluminum foil and cook in the water bath to an internal temperature of 135°F/57°C for seafood, 145°F/63°C for pork or veal, or 160°F/71°C for chicken. Remove the terrine from the water bath. When it's cool enough to handle, weight the terrine (see page 30) and refrigerate until thoroughly chilled. Unmold, slice, and serve (see page 30).

YIELD: 15 APPETIZER PORTIONS

TEMPERATURE PLAYS A CRITICAL ROLE IN THE SUCCESS OF ALL FORCEMEAT.

Chicken and Wild Mushroom Terrine

(MASTER MOUSSELINE FORCEMEAT RECIPE)

This is a delicious terrine made from the most common ingredients—boneless chicken and mushrooms. And yet when you handle these prosaic ingredients in the right way, to make a flavorful mousseline, it's a sight to behold and a marvel to eat.

Use a light brush to clean the mushrooms of all dirt and debris rather than washing them under water because they will absorb that water and dilute their flavor.

2 tablespoons unsalted butter

12 ounces/340 grams fresh wild or cultivated mushrooms (such as morels, chanterelles, creminis, and/or shiitakes), cut into medium to large dice

¼ cup/60 milliliters Madeira wine or dry sherry

1 pound/450 grams boneless, skinless chicken meat (a mix of breast and thigh), trimmed and cut into ½-inch/1-centimeter dice

2 large egg whites

1 tablespoon/15 grams kosher salt

1 teaspoon ground white pepper

½ teaspoon grated nutmeg

¾ cup/180 milliliters heavy cream

2 tablespoons chopped fresh tarragon

1 tablespoon minced fresh flat-leaf parsley

1 tablespoon sliced fresh chives

1. Prepare a water bath in a 300°F/150°C oven (see page 29).

2. In a medium sauté pan, melt the butter over medium heat. Before it browns, add the mushrooms. Cook until the moisture comes out and is almost evaporated, then add the wine and cook until dry. Remove the pan from the heat and set aside to cool.

3. In a chilled food processor bowl fitted with a chilled blade, combine the diced chicken meat, egg whites, salt, pepper, and nutmeg. Process until the mixture is smooth, about 1 minute. Scrape down the sides of the bowl once to ensure even mixing. While the machine is running, add the cream in a slow but steady stream.

4. Do a quenelle test (see page 28) and adjust the seasoning if necessary, remembering that cooked food served cold requires more seasoning.

5. Transfer the mixture to a mixing bowl. Using a rubber spatula, fold in the mushrooms and herbs.

6. Line a 1½-quart/1.5-liter terrine mold with plastic wrap and fill it with the mousseline. Fold the plastic wrap over the top.

7. Cover with a lid or aluminum foil and cook in the water bath to an internal temperature of 160°F/71°C, 45 to 60 minutes. When it's cool enough to handle, weight the terrine (see page 30) and refrigerate until thoroughly chilled. Unmold, slice, and serve (see page 30).

YIELD: 15 APPETIZER PORTIONS

VARIATION:
To Cook Mousseline as a Roulade

1. Bring a large pot of water to 180°F/82°C.

2. Once you have folded the mushrooms and herbs into the mousseline, spread out a sheet of plastic wrap about 18 inches/46 centimeters long (it helps to sprinkle your counter with water first, which makes the plastic adhere to the counter). Spatula out the mousseline into a log in the center of the plastic, about 12 inches/30 centimeters long, then roll the plastic around the mousseline into a tight cylinder, about 4 inches/10 centimeters in diameter (or whatever diameter you wish). Twist the ends to tighten the roulade, then tie them off by knotting each end of the plastic wrap. Rewrap in a second layer of plastic wrap to reinforce the shape, tightening and tying off the ends.

3. Poach the roulade in the pot of water, weighting it down with a plate to ensure that it is completely submerged, until the internal temperature is 160°F/71°C, about 1 hour. Transfer to an ice bath until thoroughly chilled. Unwrap, slice, and serve.

Meat, Seafood, and Vegetable Pâtés

＊⟶⟶⟶·⟵⟶⟶·⟵⟵⟵＊

Smoked Salmon and Dill Terrine	Lobster and Leeks en Gelée	Summer Vegetable Terrine
—	—	—
78	84	91
Lobster Terrine	**Smoked Ruby Trout en Gelée**	**Cauliflower, Pea, and Red Pepper Mousse en Terrine**
—	—	—
79	87	92
Chicken and Shrimp Terrine with Chipotle and Cilantro	**Shrimp, Scallop, and Saffron Terrine**	**Portobello and Roasted Red Pepper Terrine**
—	—	—
82	89	94
Atlantic Coast Seafood Roulade with Smoked Scallops	**Smoked Whitefish Terrine**	**Two-Potato Terrine**
—	—	—
83	90	96

Alsatian Veal and Chicken Terrine

This is a coarsely ground, heavily garnished terrine flavored with a good Alsatian white wine. Alsace is a wine-rich region in France, near the German border, that grows predominately Riesling and Gewürztraminer. Either wine can be used in this recipe; Riesling is generally the sweeter of the two, but both tend to have a sweetness characteristic of the region. The meat should marinate in the wine for 24 hours, giving this terrine its distinctive character. Note that this terrine gets a smoky flavor from the bacon, the only fat added. The terrine's richness comes, too, from the sweetbreads and liver, and the onion adds a lot of moisture.

4 ounces/110 grams slab bacon, cut into lardons

½ cup/110 grams julienned sweet onion

2 tablespoons minced shallot

6 ounces/170 grams veal sweetbreads

1 tablespoon unsalted butter

4 ounces/110 grams chanterelle mushrooms, cut into 1-inch/2.5-centimeter pieces

¼ cup fresh flat-leaf parsley, coarsely chopped

12 ounces/340 grams veal breast, cut into 1-inch/2.5-centimeter dice

6 ounces/170 grams boneless, skinless chicken breast, cut into ½-inch/1-centimeter dice

6 ounces/170 grams foie gras or chicken livers, veins and connective tissue removed, cut into 1-inch/2.5-centimeter dice

1 tablespoon sugar

1 tablespoon/15 grams kosher salt

1 teaspoon freshly ground black pepper

½ cup/120 milliliters white Alsatian wine (Riesling or Gewürztraminer)

2 large eggs, beaten

2 tablespoons all-purpose flour

Day One

1. In a sauté pan, cook the bacon lardons over medium-low heat, but don't allow them to become crisp. When they are tender and have rendered their fat, about 20 minutes, add the onion and shallot, cover the pan, and cook until the onion is very soft, even a little brown. Transfer to a bowl, set aside to cool, then chill completely in the refrigerator.

2. Meanwhile, put the sweetbreads in a saucepan, cover with water, and bring to a boil. Reduce the heat and simmer the sweetbreads for 3 minutes. Drain, allow them to cool, then remove the thick skin and any fat with a paring knife. Break the sweetbreads into ½-inch/1-centimeter pieces.

3. Melt the butter in a sauté pan over medium-high heat. Add the sweetbreads and brown them. Add the chanterelles and sauté until soft. Remove from the heat, add the parsley, and set aside to cool.

4. Combine the veal breast with the chilled bacon and onion mixture. Grind it all through a ⅜-inch/9-millimeter die into a metal bowl set in an ice bath. Add the diced chicken breast, foie gras, and cooled sweetbread mixture. Season with the sugar, salt, and pepper. Add the wine, mix to distribute all the ingredients, then cover with plastic wrap and refrigerate for 24 hours.

Day Two

1. Prepare a water bath in a 300°F/150°C oven (see page 29).

2. Remove the meat mixture from the refrigerator, add the eggs and flour, and mix well by hand. Do a quenelle test (see page 28) and adjust seasonings if necessary, remembering that cooked food served cold requires more seasoning.

3. Line a 1½-quart/1.5-liter terrine mold with plastic wrap and fill it with the pâté. Fold the plastic wrap over the top.

4. Cover with a lid or aluminum foil and cook in the water bath to an internal temperature of 160°F/71°C, 45 to 60 minutes. Remove the terrine from the water bath. When it's cool enough to handle, weight the terrine (see page 30) and refrigerate until thoroughly chilled. Unmold, slice, and serve (see page 30).

YIELD: 15 APPETIZER PORTIONS

Asian-Spiced Pâté

The seasoning profile of this pork terrine lends itself to a bánh mì, the traditional Vietnamese sandwich. Originally, chicken liver pâté was used, but if you make this pâté, use the leftovers and end cuts in the sandwich. Serve with the appropriate condiments, such as Chinese mustard, kimchi, pickled ginger, and wasabi.

1½ pounds/680 grams pork shoulder, cut into 1-inch/2.5-centimeter dice

1 pound/450 grams pork back fat, cut into 1-inch/2.5-centimeter dice

1 pound/450 grams chicken livers, veins and connective tissue removed, cut into 1-inch/2.5-centimeter dice

2 scallions (white and pale green parts only), minced

1 tablespoon minced garlic

1 tablespoon minced shallot

1 tablespoon grated fresh ginger

1 large egg, beaten

¼ cup/60 milliliters fish sauce

2 tablespoons brandy

2 tablespoons/ 30 grams kosher salt

1 tablespoon sugar

1 tablespoon five-spice powder (see Note)

2 teaspoons freshly ground black pepper

---

1. Prepare a water bath in a 300°F/150°C oven (see page 29).

2. Combine the pork shoulder and back fat and grind through a ¼-inch/6-millimeter die into a metal bowl set in an ice bath. Transfer one-third of this mixture to the grinding tray, add the chicken livers, and grind through a ⅛-inch/3-millimeter die.

3. Add the remaining ingredients to the ground meat and mix until all the ingredients are evenly distributed.

4. Line a 1½-quart/1.5-liter terrine mold with plastic wrap and fill it with the pâté. Fold the plastic wrap over the top.

5. Cover with a lid or aluminum foil and cook in the water bath to an internal temperature of 145°F/63°C. Remove the terrine from the water bath. When it's cool enough to handle, weight the terrine (see page 30) and refrigerate until thoroughly chilled. Unmold, slice, and serve (see page 30).

YIELD: 15 APPETIZER PORTIONS

FIVE-SPICE POWDER is a very aromatic seasoning used in many Asian dishes. It's commonly available in the spice section of your grocery store. If you want to make your own, here is our base formula:

2 ounces/60 grams star anise, roughly chopped

1 ounce/30 grams fennel seeds

½ ounce/15 grams whole cloves

½ ounce/15 grams Szechwan peppercorns

2 ounces/60 grams ground cinnamon

Toast the star anise, fennel, cloves, and peppercorns together in a dry sauté pan over medium heat until the spices become fragrant. Add the cinnamon and grind in a spice grinder. Store in an airtight container at room temperature for up to 2 months.

YIELD: ¾ CUP/180 GRAMS

Terrine Bordelaise

Similar to the Alsatian terrine, this farce is flavored with wine—here, the rich red wine of the Bordeaux region in southwestern France. In Bordeaux, winemakers grow both red and white grapes. The red varietals that work best in this recipe are Cabernet Sauvignon and Cabernet Franc, both powerful grapes of this famous region that will add richness and color to this terrine and pair well with the mushrooms.

1½ pounds/680 grams meaty pork shoulder, cut into 1-inch/2.5-centimeter dice

12 ounces/340 grams pork livers, veins and connective tissue removed, cut into 1-inch/2.5-centimeter dice

1 tablespoon/15 grams kosher salt

1 teaspoon freshly ground black pepper

1 tablespoon sugar

½ cup/120 milliliters red Bordeaux wine

1 tablespoon unsalted butter

4 ounces/110 grams fresh button mushrooms, cut into quarters

4 ounces/110 grams fresh porcini mushrooms (cepes), cut into 1-inch/2.5-centimeter pieces

2 tablespoons minced shallot

¼ cup fresh flat-leaf parsley, coarsely chopped

6 ounces/170 grams foie gras or chicken livers, veins and connective tissue removed, cut into 1-inch/2.5-centimeter dice

¼ cup/60 milliliters heavy cream

2 large eggs, beaten

2 tablespoons all-purpose flour

Day One

1. Season the pork shoulder and livers with the salt, pepper, and sugar and grind through a ⅜-inch/9-millimeter die into a metal bowl set in an ice bath.

2. Mix in the wine, cover with plastic wrap, and refrigerate overnight.

Day Two

1. Prepare a water bath in a 300°F/150°C oven (see page 29).

2. Melt the butter in a sauté pan over medium-high heat and sear the mushrooms, being careful not to overload the pan—a little browning is good here. Add the shallot and cook until soft, a minute longer. Remove the pan from the heat, add the parsley, and set aside to cool.

3. Remove the ground meat from the refrigerator and add the foie gras, cooled mushrooms, cream, eggs, and flour. Mix well by hand.

4. Do a quenelle test (see page 28) and adjust the seasoning if necessary, remembering that cooked food served cold requires extra attention.

5. Line a 1½-quart/1.5-liter terrine mold with plastic wrap and fill it with the pâté. Fold the plastic wrap over the top.

6. Cover with a lid or aluminum foil and cook in the water bath to an internal temperature of 145°F/63°C, 45 to 60 minutes. Remove the terrine from the water bath. When it's cool enough to handle, weight the terrine (see page 30) and refrigerate until thoroughly chilled. Unmold, slice, and serve (see page 30).

YIELD: 15 APPETIZER PORTIONS

CURRIED CHICKEN TERRINE SERVED WITH MANGO,
GINGER, AND JALAPEÑO CHUTNEY (PAGE 234)

Curried Chicken Terrine

Chicken and curry are, of course, a great pair, whether as a salad or a terrine. Here the diced chicken stays white in the curried farce for a dramatic visual appearance. Start this at least one day before you want to cook it; you can grind and season the meat up to three days before completing the terrine.

12 ounces/340 grams boneless, skinless chicken thighs, cut into 1-inch/2.5-centimeter dice

12 ounces/340 grams fresh pork belly, skin removed, cut into 2-inch/5-centimeter dice

4 ounces/110 grams chicken livers, veins and connective tissue removed, cut into 1-inch/2.5-centimeter dice

3 ounces/85 grams slab bacon, roughly chopped

2 tablespoons madras curry powder

1 tablespoon/15 grams kosher salt, plus more as needed

1½ teaspoon freshly ground black pepper

½ cup/120 milliliters brandy

8 ounces/225 grams boneless, skinless chicken breast, cut into 1-inch/2.5-centimeter dice

1 tablespoon unsalted butter

1 tablespoon minced shallot

4 ounces/110 grams button mushrooms, quartered

3 tablespoons chopped fresh flat leaf parsley

2 large eggs, beaten

¼ cup/60 milliliters heavy cream

Caul fat as needed (see page 137), optional

1. Combine the chicken thighs, pork belly, chicken livers, bacon, curry powder, salt, pepper, and half of the brandy in a bowl and toss to combine. Grind it all through a ⅜-inch/9-millimeter die into a metal bowl set in an ice bath. Cover with plastic wrap and refrigerate for at least 8 hours and up to 72 hours.

2. When you're ready to make the terrine, prepare a water bath in a 300°F/150°C oven (see page 29).

3. Season the chicken breast generously with salt. Melt the butter in a sauté pan over medium-high heat and sear the chicken on all sides, just enough to brown the chicken but leaving the interior raw. Transfer the chicken to a paper towel–lined plate, cover, and refrigerate. Add the shallot to the same pan and sauté just to soften, a minute or so. Add the mushrooms and sauté until cooked through, a couple of minutes, seasoning them with salt. Add the parsley, then add the remaining brandy. Reduce the liquid in the pan to a syrup consistency (you can flame the brandy if you wish!). Transfer the mixture to a bowl, cover, and refrigerate.

4. Regrind the chilled curry meat through a ⅛-inch/3-millimeter die into the bowl of a standing mixer set in an ice bath. Fit the bowl into the standing mixer and, using the paddle attachment, mix at low speed, adding the eggs and cream.

RECIPE CONTINUES ➤

5. Add the garnish of chicken breast and mushrooms and mix until everything is uniformly incorporated.

6. Line a 1½-quart/1.5-liter terrine mold with caul fat (if using) or plastic wrap and fill it with the pâté. Fold the caul fat or plastic wrap over the top.

7. Cover with a lid or aluminum foil and cook in the water bath to an internal temperature of 160°F/71°C, 45 to 60 minutes. Remove the terrine from the water bath. When it's cool enough to handle, weight the terrine (see page 30) and refrigerate until thoroughly chilled. Unmold, slice, and serve (see page 30).

YIELD: 15 APPETIZER PORTIONS

Chicken Liver Terrine

This is a simple chicken liver terrine with a sliceable custard-like texture, brightened with orange zest. As with all chicken liver preparations, particularly where the liver is the main ingredient, the quality of the livers is paramount. If you have access to local, farm-raised chickens, ask the farmer for the livers. Standard commodity livers offered in the grocery store are of uneven quality. High-quality livers can be eaten medium-rare.

1 pound/450 grams chicken livers, veins and connective tissue removed

4 large eggs

¾ cup/180 milliliters Madeira wine

2 tablespoons grated orange zest

Pinch sugar

Kosher salt and freshly ground black pepper to taste

2 cups/480 milliliters heavy cream

1. Prepare a water bath in a 300°F/150°C oven (see page 29).

2. Combine the livers, eggs, wine, zest, sugar, and salt and pepper in a food processor and puree until smooth. With the motor running, slowly pour in the cream in a steady stream until all the cream has been incorporated into the mixture.

3. Pass the liver mixture through a fine-mesh strainer.

4. Line a 1-quart/1-liter terrine mold with plastic wrap and pour the liver mixture into the mold. Fold the plastic wrap over the top.

5. Cover with a lid or aluminum foil and cook in the water bath to an internal temperature of 145°F/63°C, 45 to 60 minutes. Remove the terrine from the water bath. When it's cool enough to handle, weight the terrine (see page 30) and refrigerate until thoroughly chilled. Unmold, slice, and serve (see page 30).

YIELD: 8 APPETIZER PORTIONS

SMOKED CHICKEN LIVER TERRINE WITH INTERIOR
GARNISH OF GREEN PEPPERCORNS, PISTACHIOS,
AND SHIITAKE MUSHROOMS, SERVED WITH ONION
MARMALADE (PAGE 232)

Smoked Chicken Liver Terrine

Brian has been making this terrine for twenty-five years, with countless variations. The combination of light smoke and liver is especially appealing. Chicken livers are far more palatable to the American diet than the more mineral-y pork or calf's liver. But then, liver is liver, unique in flavor and texture. It's a valuable ingredient in terms of increasing not only flavor in a terrine but also moisture. This recipe involves a few more steps beyond the season-puree-cook method fundamental to most terrines. First, note that the livers should be combined with the milk and salt and the pork tossed with seasonings a day before cooking. Then, half the livers are cold-smoked; if you don't have the capacity to cold-smoke, this terrine is still worth making. The recipe also includes pork and fat, piquant seasonings, and several different interior garnishes. But it's worth the extra steps and ingredients, especially when you acknowledge that you are taking one of the least expensive, least desirable parts of the animal and, through your craft, making it uncommonly delicious.

1½ pounds/680 grams chicken livers, veins and connective tissue removed

2 cups/480 milliliters whole milk

2 tablespoons/30 grams kosher salt, plus more as needed

12 ounces/340 grams pork butt, cut into 1-inch/2.5-centimeter dice

12 ounces/340 grams pork back fat, cut into 1-inch/2.5-centimeter dice

2 teaspoons paprika

½ teaspoon dried thyme

¼ teaspoon ground ginger

All-Purpose Spice Mix for Meat Pâtés (page 33) to taste

Freshly ground black pepper to taste

1 tablespoon unsalted butter

2 tablespoons minced shallot

2 tablespoons minced garlic

8 ounces/225 grams fresh mushrooms (such as chanterelles, hedgehogs, and/or shiitakes), cut into large chunks

½ cup/120 milliliters brandy

1 cup/240 milliliters heavy cream

1 large egg

1 (1½-ounce/42-gram) slice crustless white bread

1 tablespoon brined green peppercorns, rinsed and drained

6 ounces/170 grams shelled pistachios

RECIPE CONTINUES ➤

1. Combine the livers, milk, and salt in a bowl or plastic bag and refrigerate for at least 12 hours and up to 24 hours.

2. In a bowl, toss the pork butt and fat with the paprika, thyme, ginger, spice mix, and salt and pepper. Cover and refrigerate for at least 12 hours and up to 24 hours.

3. Drain the chicken livers and rinse under running water, then pat dry (discard the milk). Put half of the livers in a bowl, cover, and refrigerate. Cold-smoke the remaining livers for 1 hour, making sure the temperature of the smoker does not exceed 90°F/32°C.

4. Prepare a water bath in a 300°F/150°C oven (see page 29).

5. Melt the butter in a sauté pan over medium-high heat. Add the smoked livers and brown them, leaving the centers raw. Transfer them to a paper towel–lined plate to cool, then cut into 1-inch/2.5-centimeter dice.

6. Add the shallot and garlic to the same pan and sweat the aromatics until soft, 30 seconds or so. Add the mushrooms and cook until the liquid they release is almost cooked off, then deglaze the pan with the brandy. Reduce the brandy until the pan is almost dry. Set the pan aside to cool.

7. In a bowl, beat the cream and egg together, then soak the bread in the mixture, allowing it to completely absorb the liquid.

8. Grind the marinated pork butt and fat, reserved refrigerated livers, and soaked bread through a ⅛-inch/3-millimeter die into a metal bowl set in an ice bath.

9. Transfer the ground meat to a food processor, puree it until smooth, then return it to the bowl, still in its ice bath.

10. Do a quenelle test (see page 28) and adjust the seasoning if necessary, remembering that cooked food served cold requires extra attention.

11. Fold the cooked mushrooms, green peppercorns, and pistachios into the puree.

12. Line a 1½-quart/1.5-liter terrine mold with plastic wrap and fill it halfway with the pâté. Lay the smoked livers down the center, then fill the mold with the remaining pâté. Fold the plastic wrap over the top.

13. Cover with a lid or aluminum foil and cook in the water bath to an internal temperature of 145°F/63°C, 45 to 60 minutes. Remove the terrine from the water bath. When it's cool enough to handle, weight the terrine (see page 30) and refrigerate until thoroughly chilled. Unmold, slice, and serve (see page 30).

YIELD: 12 APPETIZER PORTIONS

Chicken and Veal Terrine with Sweetbreads and Mushrooms

This is a very elegant, refined terrine, using a forcemeat of chicken and veal—use lean veal from breast, hind leg, or any less expensive cut—flavored by smoky bacon to carry a big interior garnish of sautéed chicken livers, sweetbreads, and mushrooms, all flavored with a traditional reduction of white and Madeira wines. It includes one last technique that can be employed in any farce containing cream: Rather than streaming the cream into the running food processor, it's whipped and then folded into the meat, which lightens the texture of the finished terrine.

14 ounces/400 grams lean veal meat, cut into 1-inch/2.5-centimeter dice

7 ounces/200 grams boneless, skinless chicken breast, cut into 1-inch/2.5-centimeter dice

Kosher salt to taste

7 ounces/200 grams slab bacon, cut into 1-inch/2.5-centimeter dice

7 ounces/200 grams chicken livers, veins and connective tissue removed

Freshly ground black pepper to taste

1 tablespoon vegetable oil

10 ounces/280 grams button mushrooms, quartered

2 tablespoons minced shallot

¼ cup/60 milliliters Madeira wine

¼ cup/60 milliliters dry white wine

1 large egg

2 teaspoons All-Purpose Spice Mix for Meat Pâtés (page 33)

¾ cup/180 milliliters heavy cream

7 ounces/200 grams cooked sweetbreads (see page 65), broken into 1-inch/2.5-centimeter pieces

1. Prepare a water bath in a 300°F/150°C oven (see page 29).

2. Season the veal and chicken with salt and combine it with the bacon. Grind through a ⅛-inch/3-millimeter die into a metal bowl set in an ice bath. Cover and refrigerate.

3. Season the chicken livers with salt and pepper. In a sauté pan, heat the oil over high heat. Sear the livers on both sides, leaving the centers raw. Cut them in half or into 1-inch/2.5-centimeter pieces. Transfer them to a paper towel–lined plate, cover, and refrigerate.

4. In the same pan, sauté the mushrooms until they're soft and the liquid they release has evaporated. Transfer them to a plate, cover, and refrigerate.

5. In the same pan, sauté the shallot until soft. Deglaze the pan with the Madeira and white wines. Reduce to a syrup, then transfer to a bowl, cover, and refrigerate.

6. In the bowl of a chilled food processor, combine the ground meat, egg, and chilled wine reduction. Season with the spice mix and salt and pepper. Puree until smooth.

7. Do a quenelle test (see page 28) and adjust the seasoning if necessary, remembering that cooked food served cold requires extra attention.

RECIPE CONTINUES ↱

8. Lightly whip the cream to soft peaks and gently fold it into the meat mixture. Fold in the sweetbreads, chicken livers, and mushrooms.

9. Line a 1½-quart/1.5-liter terrine mold with plastic wrap and fill it with the pâté. Fold the plastic wrap over the top.

10. Cover with a lid or aluminum foil and cook in the water bath to an internal temperature of 145°F/63°C, 45 to 60 minutes. Remove the terrine from the water bath. When it's cool enough to handle, weight the terrine (see page 30) and refrigerate until thoroughly chilled. Unmold, slice, and serve (see page 30).

YIELD: 15 APPETIZER SERVINGS

ON COOKING SWEETBREADS

Sweetbreads, the thymus gland of young cows, are part of the great category we call offal (organs and glands that are delicious and nutritious when properly prepared). They are used often as a garnish in this book because they're mild enough to take on other flavors well and, when sautéed, can be crispy on the outside and densely tender within.

They are very easy to cook, though they are almost always cooked twice—first to cook them through and make any membrane and connective tissue easy to identify and remove, and second to flavor them and give them their texture. The first cooking can be as simple as boiling them for a few minutes (see the Alsatian Veal and Chicken Terrine, page 52). But for more flavor and a terrific all-around preparation to either include in a terrine or to sauté till browned and crisp, we offer the following general technique.

¼ cup/60 grams kosher salt

1 quart/1 liter water

1 pound/450 grams sweetbreads

2 tablespoons unsalted butter

½ cup/70 grams diced onion

¼ cup diced celery

¼ cup diced parsnip

1 cup/240 milliliters Madeira wine

5 black peppercorns

½ bunch fresh thyme

1 bay leaf

1. Dissolve the salt in the water in a large bowl. Add the sweetbreads, cover, and refrigerate for 12 to 48 hours to extract any blood.

2. Drain and rinse the sweetbreads. Put them in a pot, cover them with fresh water, and bring the water to a simmer over high heat. Lower the heat and cook the sweetbreads until firm, about 15 minutes. Drain them and cool under cold running water. Remove any membrane, gristle, or other connective tissue.

3. In a sauté pan, melt the butter over medium heat. Add the onion, celery, and parsnip and cook until tender, a couple of minutes. Add the Madeira, peppercorns, thyme, and bay leaf. Nestle the sweetbreads in the liquid. When the liquid returns to a simmer, turn the heat to low, cover the pan, and braise for 20 to 30 minutes.

4. Let the sweetbreads cool in the pan. They are now ready to finish in whatever way you wish. For use as a garnish in a terrine, remove them and break or cut them into 1-inch/2.5-centimeter pieces. Strain the braising liquid and reduce for use in pâté recipes in which sweetbreads are an interior garnish.

Makes enough garnish for 1 standard terrine

CHICKEN, PORK, LIVER, AND
MUSHROOM TERRINE, SERVED
WITH WHOLE-GRAIN MUSTARD
(PAGE 228)

Chicken, Pork, Liver, and Mushroom Terrine

Brian modeled this terrine after those by the French master charcutier, Gilles Vérot, who has a number of charcuteries, called Maison Vérot, in Paris and Lyon (all of which we can't recommend more highly). This terrine is characterized by a big and abundant interior garnish of liver, chicken, and mushrooms encased in a smooth pork forcemeat—a dynamic combination of flavors.

Make sure to use fatty pork shoulder for a rich pâté. The livers should be left whole for a large interior garnish; be sure to mix the chicken breast, seared livers, and cooked mushrooms thoroughly to create a compelling mosaic. The cream is folded in by hand so that the forcemeat doesn't become overly aerated. Serve this pâté with the customary condiments and greens.

14 ounces/400 grams fatty pork shoulder, cut into 2-inch/5-centimeter dice

Kosher salt and freshly ground black pepper to taste

9 ounces/255 grams chicken livers, veins and connective tissue removed

1 to 2 tablespoons vegetable oil or lard

3 ounces/85 grams mixed fresh mushrooms (such as shiitake, oyster, chanterelle, and/or trumpet), roughly cut into ½-inch/1-centimeter pieces

¼ cup minced shallot

1 cup/240 milliliters Madeira wine

2 large eggs

2 teaspoons All-Purpose Spice Mix for Meat Pâtés (page 33)

½ cup/120 milliliters heavy cream

14 ounces/400 grams boneless, skinless chicken breast, cut crosswise into 1-inch/2.5-centimeter slices

——

1. Liberally season the pork shoulder with salt and pepper and grind it through a ⅛-inch/3-millimeter die into a metal bowl set in an ice bath. Cover and refrigerate until needed.

2. Season the chicken livers with salt and pepper. Heat 1 tablespoon oil in a sauté pan over medium-high heat and sear the livers, but do not cook through (the interior should remain raw). Cut the livers in half or into 1-inch/2.5-centimeter pieces. Transfer them to a paper towel–lined plate, cover, and refrigerate until they're thoroughly chilled.

3. In the same pan, sauté the mushrooms and shallot over medium-high heat, adding more oil as needed. Deglaze with the Madeira. When the mushrooms are soft, transfer them to a bowl and refrigerate until they're thoroughly chilled. Reduce the liquid in the pan to a syrup, transfer it to a ramekin, and refrigerate until chilled.

4. Prepare a water bath in a 300°F/150°C oven (see page 29).

RECIPE CONTINUES ↻

5. In a chilled food processor bowl with a chilled blade, puree the pork, eggs, Madeira reduction, spice mix, and salt and pepper until smooth.

6. Do a quenelle test (see page 28) and adjust the seasoning if necessary, remembering that cooked food served cold requires extra attention.

7. Fold in the cream by hand, then fold in the seared liver, mushrooms, and chicken breast.

8. Line a 1½-quart/1.5-liter terrine mold with plastic wrap and fill it with the pâté, packing it down to eliminate any air pockets. Fold the plastic wrap over the top.

9. Cover with a lid or aluminum foil and cook in the water bath to an internal temperature of 160°F/71°C, 45 to 60 minutes. Remove the terrine from the water bath. When it's cool enough to handle, weight the terrine (see page 30) and refrigerate until thoroughly chilled. Unmold, slice, and serve (see page 30).

YIELD: 15 APPETIZER PORTIONS

Pork Liver Terrine

This light, custard-like recipe uses the liver in an elegant way, its flavor balanced with citrus zest, garlic, and shallot and enriched with abundant cream (notice equal parts cream and liver). As more and more chefs practice farm-to-table cooking, it's important that they know how to make offal appeal to a broad audience. This is one way of working with the excellent and nutritious pork liver. Pickled vegetables and arugula go particularly well with it.

1 tablespoon vegetable oil

2 tablespoons minced garlic

2 tablespoons minced shallot

1 pound/450 grams pork liver, veins and connective tissue removed

½ cup/115 grams unsalted butter, at room temperature

4 large eggs

¾ cup/180 milliliters Sauternes

2 tablespoons/30 milliliters brandy

2 tablespoons grated orange zest

2 tablespoons grated lemon zest

1 tablespoon sugar

2 teaspoons ground juniper berries

1 teaspoon/5 grams kosher salt

2 cups/480 milliliters heavy cream

1. Prepare a water bath in a 300°F/150°C oven (see page 29).

2. In a sauté pan, heat the oil over medium heat. Sauté the garlic and shallot gently until they're translucent, a minute or so. Remove the pan from the heat and allow to cool. Transfer to a food processor.

3. Add all the remaining ingredients except the cream to the food processor and puree until smooth. Slowly add the cream while the machine is running— the mixture will lighten in color.

4. Pass the mixture through a fine-mesh sieve.

5. Line a 1½-quart/1.5 liter terrine mold with plastic wrap and fill it with the pâté. Fold the plastic wrap over the top.

6. Cover with a lid or aluminum foil and cook it in the water bath to an internal temperature of 145°F/63°C, 45 to 60 minutes. Remove the terrine from the water bath. When it is cool enough to handle, weight the terrine (see page 30) and refrigerate until thoroughly chilled. Unmold, slice, and serve (see page 30).

YIELD: 15 APPETIZER PORTIONS

SPICY MOROCCAN LAMB TERRINE
WITH ROASTED RED PEPPERS

Spicy Moroccan Lamb Terrine with Roasted Red Peppers

Every culture has a form of baked cooked ground meats. No matter where you go, the principles are the same: Meat, fat, seasonings, and often an interior garnish (here, roasted peppers) come together in a delicious regional pâté. This one is no different. We're not big fans of lamb fat, which can be waxy and have a gamy flavor, so we use clean, neutral pork fat here. The basic procedure is the same as making a Country Pâté (page 44), using two different-size grinds for texture.

Aleppo is a mildly spicy, fruity pepper that grows in Turkey and Syria and is often used in Mediterranean cuisines. It's worth seeking out, but if you can't find it, try using ancho chile powder instead.

1 pound/450 grams boneless lean lamb shoulder or shank, free of heavy sinew, cut into 1-inch/2.5-centimeter dice

8 ounces/225 grams pork back fat, cut into 1-inch/2.5-centimeter dice

2 tablespoons chopped fresh flat-leaf parsley

2 tablespoons chopped fresh oregano

1 tablespoon minced garlic

1½ tablespoons/22 grams kosher salt

1 tablespoon ground Aleppo pepper or ancho chile powder

1 tablespoon ground coriander

2 teaspoons freshly ground black pepper

¼ teaspoon pink curing salt, optional

¼ cup/60 milliliters heavy cream

1 large egg

3 tablespoons all-purpose flour

2 red bell peppers, roasted, peeled, seeded, patted dry, and cut into ¼-inch/6-millimeter dice

12 ounces/340 grams cooked and/or smoked lamb or pork tongue, peeled and cut into ⅓-inch/8-millimeter dice

———

1. Combine the lamb, pork fat, parsley, oregano, garlic, kosher salt, Aleppo pepper, coriander, black pepper, and pink salt (if using) in a bowl. Toss it all together well, cover the bowl with plastic wrap, and refrigerate for 8 to 24 hours.

2. Prepare a water bath in a 300°F/150°C oven (see page 29).

3. Grind the meat-fat-spice mixture through a ¼-inch/6-millimeter die into a metal bowl set in an ice bath. Replace the die with a ⅛-inch/3-millimeter die and regrind one-third of the ground meat into the bowl, still in its ice bath. Combine the two grinds and refrigerate.

4. In a small bowl, whisk together the cream, egg, and flour. Add it to the meat mixture and stir with a wooden spoon or spatula until thoroughly incorporated.

5. Do a quenelle test (see page 28) and adjust the seasoning if necessary, remembering that cooked food served cold requires extra attention.

RECIPE CONTINUES ➲

6. Fold in the garnish of roasted peppers and tongue.

7. Line a 1½-quart/1.5-liter terrine mold with plastic wrap and fill it with the pâté, packing it into the mold tightly. Fold the plastic wrap over the top.

8. Cover with a lid or aluminum foil and cook in the water bath to an internal temperature of 145°F/63°C, 45 to 60 minutes. Remove the terrine from the water bath. When it's cool enough to handle, weight the terrine (see page 30) and refrigerate until thoroughly chilled. Unmold, slice, and serve (see page 30).

YIELD: 15 APPETIZER PORTIONS

Gratin of Rabbit with Apricots and Armagnac

That we like dried fruit especially in game pâtés or any powerfully flavored protein is intuitive. But dried fruit—here, marinated dried fruit—also complements the neutral flavor of rabbit, which we consider an underused meat. We would love to encourage more home cooks to make rabbit an occasional menu choice. Rabbit and prunes are a common and symbiotic pairing, which was what Brian had planned to make when he began to develop this recipe. But on that day he found that he had no prunes. He did have apricots, though, and since apricots are in the same family as plums, he gave it a shot. And it turns out that apricots are better than prunes, and brighter.

This recipe calls for 12 ounces/340 grams of lean leg meat; 2 hind legs should weigh about 1 pound/450 grams and give you the amount you need. If you're a little short, supplement with extra pork butt. We encourage you to buy a whole rabbit and cook the rest of it as you would chicken—roast, sauté, or braise—and use the bones for a stock or sauce.

4 ounces/110 grams dried apricots

1 cup/240 milliliters Armagnac or brandy

2 tablespoons vegetable oil

5 ounces/140 grams slab bacon, cut into 1-inch/2.5-centimeter dice

5 ounces/140 grams pork butt, cut into 1-inch/2.5-centimeter dice

2 tablespoons minced shallot

12 ounces/340 grams lean rabbit leg meat, cut into 1-inch/2.5-centimeter dice

6 ounces/170 grams pork back fat, cut into 1-inch/2.5-centimeter dice

2 large egg whites

1½ teaspoons All-Purpose Spice Mix for Meat Pâtés (page 33)

1 tablespoon/15 grams kosher salt

Freshly ground black pepper to taste

---

1. Marinate the apricots in the brandy overnight at room temperature. Strain the apricots, reserving the brandy.

2. Prepare a water bath in a 300°F/150°C oven (see page 29).

3. Heat the vegetable oil in a sauté pan over high heat. Brown the bacon and pork butt on all sides, leaving the centers raw. Transfer the meat to a plate, cover, and refrigerate. Add the shallot to the same pan and cook until softened. Deglaze the pan with the reserved brandy. Reduce the liquid to a syrup, transfer to a ramekin, and refrigerate.

RECIPE CONTINUES ➤

4. Grind the rabbit, back fat, and browned bacon and pork butt through a ⅛-inch/3-millimeter die into a metal bowl set in an ice bath. Transfer the ground meat to a food processor and add the egg whites, chilled shallot reduction, spice mix, salt, and pepper. Puree until smooth.

5. Do a quenelle test (see page 28) and adjust the seasoning if necessary, remembering that cooked food served cold requires extra attention.

6. Cut the apricots into ¼-inch/6-millimeter dice and fold into the forcemeat.

7. Line a 1½-quart/1.5-liter terrine mold with plastic wrap and fill it with the pâté. Fold the plastic wrap over the top.

8. Cover with a lid or aluminum foil and cook in the water bath to an internal temperature of 135°F/57°C, 45 to 60 minutes. Remove the terrine from the water bath. When it's cool enough to handle, weight the terrine (see page 30) and refrigerate until thoroughly chilled. Unmold, slice, and serve (see page 30).

YIELD: 15 APPETIZER PORTIONS

GRATIN OF RABBIT WITH
APRICOTS AND ARMAGNAC (PAGE
73), SERVED WITH DRIED TART
CHERRY MARMALADE (PAGE 231)

Pheasant and Pernod Terrine with Fennel Confit

We use pheasant here because we know a lot of hunters who want to learn new ways to prepare these birds. They're so mild that it's common to let them hang for several days to develop some flavor from decomposition, but here we add our own flavors. Game generally makes a good forcemeat; because it's lean we add as much as 80 percent fat, which creates a smooth, flavorful forcemeat. In this case the licorice flavor from the Pernod and fennel confit complements the bird's natural delicacy.

1 (3-pound/1.4-kilogram) pheasant

6 ounces/170 grams pork shoulder, or more as needed

10 ounces/280 grams pork back fat, cut into 1-inch/2.5-centimeter dice

Kosher salt and freshly ground black pepper to taste

1 tablespoon vegetable oil

3 tablespoons minced garlic

3 tablespoons minced shallot

½ cup/120 milliliters Madeira wine

¼ cup/60 milliliters Pernod

1 large egg white

1 tablespoon grated orange zest

1 teaspoon ground fennel seed

12 ounces/340 grams Fennel Confit (page 178), cut into ¼-inch/6-millimeter dice

10 ounces/280 grams smoked ham or tongue, cut into ¼-inch/6-millimeter dice

1. Prepare a water bath in a 300°F/150°C oven (see page 29).

2. Bone the pheasant, leaving the breast whole. Carefully bone the legs and thighs, making sure to remove all skin and tendons. Weigh the dark meat and supplement with enough pork shoulder to yield a total of 12 ounces/340 grams. Cut the pheasant dark meat and pork shoulder into 1-inch/2.5-centimeter dice. Grind the pheasant dark meat, pork shoulder, and pork back fat through a ⅛-inch/3-millimeter die into a metal bowl set in an ice bath. Cover and refrigerate.

3. Season the pheasant breast with salt and pepper. In a sauté pan, heat the oil over high heat. Brown the breast on both sides, leaving the center raw. Transfer to a plate and refrigerate.

4. In the same pan, sauté the garlic and shallot over medium heat until tender but without color. Add the Madeira and reduce to a syrupy consistency. Set aside.

5. Combine the ground meat and fat in a food processor with the cooled Madeira reduction, Pernod, egg white, orange zest, and ground fennel seed. Puree until smooth.

6. Do a quenelle test (see page 28) and adjust the seasoning if necessary, remembering that cooked food served cold requires extra attention.

7. Fold the diced fennel confit and diced ham or tongue into the puree.

8. Line a 1½-quart/1.5-liter terrine mold with plastic wrap and fill it halfway with the pâté. Place the seared breast on top, then fill the mold with the remaining pâté. Fold the plastic wrap over the top.

9. Cover with a lid or aluminum foil and cook in the water bath to an internal temperature of 145°F/63°C, 45 to 60 minutes. Remove the terrine from the water bath. When it's cool enough to handle, weight the terrine (see page 30) and refrigerate until thoroughly chilled. Unmold, slice, and serve (see page 30).

YIELD: 15 APPETIZER PORTIONS

Smoked Salmon and Dill Terrine

This is a great starter course that has a lot of flavor and color while remaining simple: a layering of sliced zucchini, smoked salmon, and cream cheese, seasoned with fresh dill. Buy the best-quality smoked salmon available or cure and smoke your own (see our book *Charcuterie*). Dill is a natural pairing with salmon, but any combination of leafy herbs will work if you don't love dill. When building the mold, make sure all the layers are even so the finished slices are pleasing and clean looking; don't make the cream cheese layer too thick or the terrine can be difficult to slice.

2 medium (8-inch/20-centimeter) zucchini

12 ounces/340 grams cream cheese

¼ cup fresh dill

1½ pounds/680 grams sliced smoked salmon

1. Trim the ends off the zucchini and slice them lengthwise ⅛-inch/3 millimeters thick.

2. Bring a pot of salted water to a boil and prepare an ice bath. Blanch the zucchini for 20 seconds, then drain, shock in the ice bath, and pat dry.

3. Combine the cream cheese and dill in a food processor and puree until smooth.

4. Line a 2-cup/480-milliliter half-moon mold with plastic wrap. Line the interior with a layer of zucchini slices, crosswise, allowing the ends to extend up and over the edges of the mold. Spread a thin layer of cream cheese on the zucchini, then cover with a layer of smoked salmon. Repeat until the mold is full. Fold the zucchini ends over the top and cover the mold with plastic wrap. Cover and refrigerate until thoroughly chilled. Unmold, slice, and serve (see page 30).

YIELD: 8 APPETIZER PORTIONS

Lobster Terrine

The base of this elegant terrine, the forcemeat that holds the lobster, is a shrimp mousseline, which complements the lobster but also brings the overall cost down a little, as opposed to using all lobster for the farce. (The recipe calls for rock shrimp, which tend to be less expensive; regular gulf shrimp will work as well.) Keep the lobster pieces large, which will make for a dramatic presentation, as will the cooked roe if you have it. We prefer a 1-quart/1-liter mold, but the standard 1½-quart/1.5-liter terrine mold can also be used.

This is fabulous with lemon-shallot or tarragon mayonnaise and mild greens, such as mâche, or a basil cream sauce.

8 ounces/225 grams rock shrimp, peeled and deveined

1 large egg white

2 teaspoons freshly squeezed lemon juice

1 teaspoon Dijon mustard

Kosher salt and ground white pepper to taste

¾ cup/180 milliliters heavy cream

1 pound/450 grams cooked lobster meat (preferably claw and knuckle meat), cut into 1-inch/2.5-centimeter chunks

2 tablespoons lobster roe, dried and crumbled, optional (see Note)

2 tablespoons chopped fresh chives

2 tablespoons coarsely chopped fresh dill

1. Prepare a water bath in a 300°F/150°C oven (see page 29).

2. Combine the shrimp, egg white, lemon juice, mustard, and salt and pepper in the chilled bowl of a food processor with a chilled blade and pulse until smooth.

3. With the machine running, add the cream in a thin stream until all the cream has been incorporated. Remove the mousseline from the bowl and pass it through a fine-mesh sieve into a metal bowl set in an ice bath.

4. Fold the lobster, roe (if using), chives, and dill into the mousseline.

5. Line a 1-quart/1-liter terrine mold with plastic wrap and fill it with the pâté, packing it down to remove any air pockets. Fold the plastic wrap over the top.

6. Cover with a lid or aluminum foil and cook in the water bath to an internal temperature of 135°F/57°C, 30 to 45 minutes. Remove the terrine from the water bath. When it's cool enough to handle, weight the terrine (see page 30) and refrigerate until thoroughly chilled. Unmold, slice, and serve (see page 30).

YIELD: 8 APPETIZER PORTIONS

NOTE: If possible, buy female lobsters and, after poaching, remove the bright roe, sometimes called coral. Place it on a parchment-lined rimmed baking sheet and bake in a 350°F/175°C oven until dry, 10 or 15 minutes. When it's cool, crumble it into small chunks.

LOBSTER TERRINE (PAGE 79)

CHICKEN AND SHRIMP
TERRINE WITH CHIPOTLE AND
CILANTRO (PAGE 82)

Chicken and Shrimp Terrine with Chipotle and Cilantro

This terrine is a great example of the versatility of the terrine technique. It's surely never been made in France, but we love the dynamic flavor of the chipotle chile (smoked jalapeño) packed in adobo sauce—we use the sauce, seeds, and flesh of the pepper, everything. It gives color, intense smoke, and heat to the forcemeat of chicken and shrimp. Whole shrimp and cilantro make up the interior garnish, so in this case, larger shrimp are better to use here rather than the less expensive rock shrimp.

1½ pounds/680 grams boneless, skinless chicken breast, cut into ½-inch/1-centimeter dice

1 pound/450 grams shrimp, peeled, deveined, and roughly chopped

2 large egg whites

¼ cup chipotle chiles in adobo sauce

1 teaspoon/5 grams kosher salt

Pinch white pepper

Pinch grated nutmeg

¾ cup/180 milliliters heavy cream

½ cup/30 grams coarsely chopped fresh cilantro

1. Prepare a water bath in a 300°F/150°C oven (see page 29).

2. In a food processor, combine 1 pound/450 grams of the chicken, 4 ounces/110 grams of the shrimp, the egg whites, chipotles in adobo, salt, pepper, and nutmeg. Puree the mixture until all the ingredients are incorporated; with the machine running, add the cream in a thin, steady stream.

3. Do a quenelle test (see page 28) and adjust the seasoning if necessary, remembering that cooked food served cold requires extra attention. When the forcemeat tastes excellent, fold in the remaining chicken and shrimp and the cilantro.

4. Line a 1½-quart/1.5-liter terrine mold with plastic wrap and fill it with the pâté, packing it into the mold tightly. Fold the plastic wrap over the top.

5. Cover with a lid or aluminum foil and cook in the water bath to an internal temperature of 160°F/71°C, 45 to 60 minutes. When it's cool enough to handle, weight the terrine (see page 30) and refrigerate until thoroughly chilled. Unmold, slice, and serve (see page 30).

YIELD: 8 APPETIZER PORTIONS

Atlantic Coast Seafood Roulade with Smoked Scallops

This is an excellent way to utilize seafood trim in the kitchen, such as the belly and tail from round fish. Be sure to use only lean to moderately fatty fish and to trim all dark blood lines. Brian cold-smokes his scallops, but this step can be omitted and the results will still be delicious.

8 ounces/225 grams scallops

6 tablespoons/90 milliliters heavy cream

Pinch saffron

10 ounces/280 grams rock shrimp, peeled and deveined

1 large egg white

2 teaspoons/10 grams kosher salt

1 teaspoon ground white pepper

½ teaspoon grated nutmeg

8 ounces/225 grams boneless, skinless salmon, cut into ½-inch/1-centimeter dice

1 tablespoon chopped fresh flat-leaf parsley

1 tablespoon chopped fresh chervil

1. If you are smoking the scallops, place them on a rack in a cold smoker for 20 minutes. Whether smoked or not, cut the scallops into ½-inch/1-centimeter dice. Refrigerate until ready to use.

2. Heat the cream and saffron in a small saucepan to 160°F/71°C—too hot to hold your hand to but before it reaches a simmer. Remove the pan from the heat to infuse as it cools, then refrigerate to chill thoroughly.

3. Combine the rock shrimp, egg white, salt, pepper, and nutmeg in a food processor and puree until smooth. With the machine running, slowly pour in the chilled saffron cream and process until incorporated.

4. Do a quenelle test (see page 28) and adjust the seasoning if necessary, remembering that cooked food served cold requires extra attention.

5. Fold in the salmon, scallops, and herbs. Mix until all the ingredients are uniformly incorporated.

6. Lay out a piece of plastic wrap 24 by 18 inches/60 by 45 centimeters.

7. With a rubber spatula, spread the fish mixture down the middle of the plastic wrap into a log that is about 12 by 4 inches/30 by 10 centimeters. Use the plastic to roll it into a tight cylinder and twist both ends of the plastic to tighten it as much as possible, then tie off each end with a knot. Repeat with a second layer of plastic wrap to reinforce the shape. Tie the ends off in a knot or with string.

8. Bring a large pot of water 160°F/71°C, then poach the roulade to an internal temperature of 135°F/57°C, 30 to 45 minutes. Transfer to an ice bath until completely chilled. Unwrap, slice, and serve (see page 30).

YIELD: 12 APPETIZER PORTIONS

Lobster and Leeks en Gelée

A while back, Brian wanted to put a whole lobster on his menu at Five Lakes Grill in Milford, Michigan, as a special. He guessed he could sell twenty-four, so that's what he ordered. But on that Friday night, he sold only twenty. The next morning he was left with four whole lobsters. He couldn't put a lobster special on the menu to get rid of the last four; one of his knucklehead waiters was sure to sell a fifth one, he said, and he didn't want to have to 86 a special so quickly.

So, instead, he used this technique to turn those four lobsters into sixteen portions by transforming them into this terrine. The math is simple. He can buy two lobsters for $24 each ($48) and sell them for $36 each ($72), for a profit of $24. Or he can make a terrine with the two lobsters that will create eight portions at $14 each ($112) for more than triple the profit ($88).

But for our purposes, this is also just a delicious way to serve lobster to a group of people. Be sure not to overcook the lobster! Its tenderness is important to the finished terrine. Press it gently to make sure everything is evenly distributed as it chills. Serve with a mild salad of mâche and a tarragon vinaigrette.

2 live lobsters (about 1½ pounds/680 grams each)

1½ cups/360 milliliters clarified fish stock (see page 88)

¼ cup/60 milliliters cold water

1 tablespoon powdered gelatin

Kosher salt to taste

9 ounces/255 grams leeks, whites and tensder pale green parts only, cut into ¼-inch/6-millimeter pieces

2 tablespoons fresh chervil leaves

—

1. Preheat the oven to 350°F/175°C.

2. Bring a large pot of water to a boil and cook the lobsters for 7 minutes. Remove them from the water and allow to cool to room temperature.

3. Remove the meat from the shells, saving any roe if the lobsters are female. Chill the meat in the refrigerator. Discard the lungs, but reserve everything else.

4. Spread out the shells and legs and other non-meaty parts in a large roasting pan and roast until lightly browned, about 20 minutes.

5. Meanwhile, poach the roe, if any, until bright red, about a minute. Set aside.

6. Pour the clarified stock into a saucepan and add the roasted shells and legs. Simmer for 30 minutes, then strain; discard the shells and legs. Return the stock to the pan.

7. Pour the cold water into a small cup and sprinkle the gelatin over it. Let it sit for 3 to 4 minutes to bloom (that is, absorb the water without forming clumps). Add the gelatin mixture to the stock and gently warm to dissolve the gelatin. Remove from the heat and allow the aspic to cool to room temperature.

8. Bring a pot of salted water to a boil and prepare an ice bath. Blanch the leeks until they are completely tender, a minute or so. Remove them with a skimmer and plunge them into the ice bath.

9. Cut the lobster meat into ½-inch/1-centimeter dice. Combine the meat in a bowl with the leeks and chervil (and roe, if you have it). Add ½ cup/120 milliliters of the aspic and toss to evenly distribute the ingredients.

10. Line a 1-quart/1-liter terrine mold with plastic wrap and fill it with the lobster mixture. Add enough of the remaining aspic, about 1 cup/240 milliliters, so that when it's lightly pressed, the aspic rises to the height of the lobster mixture.

11. Fold the plastic wrap over the top and refrigerate until thoroughly chilled. Unmold, slice, and serve (see page 30).

YIELD: 8 APPETIZER PORTIONS

SMOKED RUBY TROUT EN GELÉE

Smoked Ruby Trout en Gelée

This terrine is all about the trout, which is smoked and bound with a gelled seafood consommé and enhanced with herbs. Ruby trout, also known as steelhead trout, is available commercially as a farm-raised fish; the best producers feed the fish a rich diet of freshwater shrimp, which lends a bright red color to the flesh of that fish. The fish itself is mild, but it accepts the exotic seasoning of smoke. This terrine also works well with wild Atlantic salmon or any other moderately fatty fish.

½ cup/120 milliliters cold water

2 tablespoons powdered gelatin

2 cups/480 milliliters clarified fish stock (see page 88)

1½ pounds/680 grams boneless, skinless smoked trout or salmon, broken into ½-inch/1-centimeter pieces

2 tablespoons coarsely chopped fresh flat-leaf parsley

1 tablespoon coarsely chopped fresh chervil

1. Pour the cold water into a small saucepan and sprinkle the gelatin over it. Let it sit for 3 to 4 minutes to bloom (that is, absorb the water without forming clumps). Add the stock and warm over medium-low heat to dissolve the gelatin. Remove from the heat and allow the aspic to cool to room temperature.

2. In a bowl, combine the fish and herbs. Add three-quarters of the aspic to the bowl and toss the fish to ensure that all pieces are coated with aspic.

3. Line a 1-quart/1-liter terrine mold with plastic wrap and fill it with the fish mixture. Pour the remaining aspic into the mold, then fold the plastic wrap over the top. Press down on the terrine until the juices rise to the top of the mold. Refrigerate until thoroughly chilled. Unmold, slice, and serve (see page 30).

YIELD: 8 APPETIZER PORTIONS

CLARIFIED STOCK FOR ASPIC

Aspic is any stock that is gelled enough to be sliceable. It's customary to clarify this stock, as you would a consommé, for an elegant appearance. It's very easy to do and also very satisfying, to take a flavorful, opaque stock and through the craft of cooking, give it even more flavor while making it crystal clear. This is done by adding egg whites to cold stock, which, when they congeal, form a "raft," a kind of net that traps all the particles that make a stock opaque. This also removes flavor from the stock, so we add meat and vegetables to give their flavor in return. The result is a flavorful consommé that can be served on its own—or, for our purposes, it is gelled and used to bind ingredients in a terrine.

12 ounces/340 grams coarsely ground lean meat (beef, chicken, veal, turkey, or monkfish, depending on the type of stock you're clarifying)

½ cup/70 grams finely chopped onion

¼ cup finely chopped carrot

¼ cup finely chopped celery

3 large egg whites

1 cup/240 milliliters Madeira wine, optional

1 Roma tomato, coarsely chopped

1 bay leaf

12 black peppercorns

1 bunch fresh thyme

5 cups/1.2 liters rich chicken, white veal, or fish stock

1. Combine all the ingredients except the stock in a thick-bottomed pot that is taller than it is wide and mix well. Add the stock and put the pan over high heat. Stir the pot gently but continuously with a flat-edged wooden spoon, making sure to keep the egg whites from sticking to the bottom of the pan. As the stock comes up to a simmer, the protein will begin to coagulate. Continue stirring only so long as it takes the protein to begin to rise as a solid raft. Turn the heat to low, just high enough that some of the stock rises over the raft and falls back through it (further clarifying), but being careful not to break the raft. Continue to cook gently for 45 minutes to an hour.

2. Ladle the consommé through a fine-mesh strainer lined with a double layer of cheesecloth or a coffee filter for perfectly clear consommé. This will keep for 1 week refrigerated or 1 month frozen.

YIELD: ABOUT 1 QUART/1 LITER

Shrimp, Scallop, and Saffron Terrine

This terrine uses a standard scallop mousseline, seasoned with white pepper and nutmeg, to suspend whole shrimp and abundant herbs (the recipe calls for a cup of chives, but feel free to use a mix of leafy herbs, such as parsley and tarragon, if you wish). The saffron-infused cream gives the mousseline a dynamic color, offsetting the pale shrimp and the green of the herbs. It's important to use fresh scallops, preferably dry-packed; scallops that have been frozen can be too watery and won't allow the mousseline to set up. Be sure to pat them dry with paper towels. Serve this terrine with a salad loaded with small-diced cucumber and tomato and a light vinaigrette.

¾ cup/180 milliliters heavy cream

Pinch saffron

1 pound/450 grams sea scallops

2 large egg whites

1 teaspoon fresh lemon juice

1 tablespoon/15 grams kosher salt

1 teaspoon ground white pepper

½ teaspoon grated nutmeg

1 pound/450 grams rock shrimp, peeled and deveined

1 cup/100 grams chopped fresh chives

1. Prepare a water bath in a 300°F/150°C oven (see page 29).

2. Heat the cream and saffron in a small saucepan to 160°F/71°C—too hot to hold your hand to but before it reaches a simmer. Remove the pan from the heat to infuse as it cools, then refrigerate to chill thoroughly.

3. Combine the scallops, egg whites, lemon juice, salt, pepper, and nutmeg in a food processor and puree until smooth. Then, with the machine running, slowly pour in the cold saffron cream and process until incorporated.

4. Do a quenelle test (see page 28) and adjust the seasoning if necessary, remembering that cooked food served cold requires extra attention.

5. Fold in the shrimp and chives. Mix until all ingredients are uniformly incorporated.

6. Line a 1½-quart/1.5-liter terrine mold with plastic wrap and fill it with the mixture. Fold the plastic wrap over the top.

7. Cover with a lid or aluminum foil and cook in the water bath to an internal temperature of 135°F/57°C, 30 to 45 minutes. Remove the terrine from the water bath. When it's cool enough to handle, weight the terrine (see page 30) and refrigerate until thoroughly chilled. Unmold, slice, and serve (see page 30).

YIELD: 15 APPETIZER PORTIONS

Smoked Whitefish Terrine

This is a great-tasting but simple terrine in which a shrimp mousseline binds smoked whitefish. It's yet another example of how important charcuterie techniques are to the modern kitchen, utilizing small pieces that aren't really enough to be useful (or interesting) on their own and transforming them into an exciting dish. Whitefish is a Great Lakes fish, part of our own Midwestern culinary heritage, but this will work with any smoked fish. If you're in New England, try it with smoked bluefish (and change the herb from dill to chive). Because of the power of the smoke, this works well with a strong sauce— add a little cream to the Horseradish-Beer Mustard (page 229) for an elegant accompaniment.

2 pounds/1 kilogram rock shrimp, peeled and deveined

1 large egg white

Juice of 1 lemon

2 teaspoons/10 grams kosher salt

1 teaspoon ground white pepper

1 cup/240 milliliters heavy cream

1 pound/450 grams smoked whitefish, flaked with a fork

1 tablespoon chopped fresh dill

1. Prepare a water bath in a 300°F/150°C oven (see page 29).

2. Combine the shrimp, egg white, lemon juice, salt, and pepper in a food processor and puree until smooth. With the machine running, slowly pour in the cream and process until incorporated.

3. Do a quenelle test (see page 28) and adjust the seasoning if necessary, remembering that cooked food served cold requires extra attention.

4. Fold in the flaked whitefish and dill.

5. Line a 1½-quart/1.5-liter terrine mold with plastic wrap and fill it with the mixture, packing it down to remove any air pockets. Fold the plastic wrap over the top.

6. Cover with a lid or aluminum foil and cook in the water bath to an internal temperature of 135°F/57°C, 30 to 45 minutes. Remove the terrine from the water bath. When it's cool enough to handle, weight the terrine (see page 30) and refrigerate until thoroughly chilled. Unmold, slice, and serve (see page 30).

YIELD: 12 APPETIZER PORTIONS

Summer Vegetable Terrine

Here a chicken mousseline is used to hold abundant vegetables and herbs. You can use any combination of vegetables in this terrine—asparagus, green beans, corn, peas—whatever is in season. Just be sure to blanch and shock them first, then pat them dry with a paper towel. If you use tomatoes, consider roasting them before seeding and dicing to concentrate their flavor.

8 ounces/225 grams zucchini, cut into ¼-inch/6-millimeter dice

8 ounces/225 grams carrots, cut into ¼-inch/6-millimeter dice

1 pound/450 grams boneless, skinless chicken breast

2 large egg whites

1 tablespoon/15 grams kosher salt

2 teaspoons ground white pepper

Pinch grated nutmeg

1 cup/240 milliliters heavy cream

8 ounces/225 grams spinach chiffonade

2 red bell peppers, roasted, peeled, seeded, and cut into ¼-inch/6-millimeter dice

½ cup/30 grams minced fresh, soft herbs (such as basil, tarragon, chives, and/or flat-leaf parsley)

1. Prepare a water bath in a 300°F/150°C oven (see page 29).

2. Bring a pot of salted water to a boil and prepare an ice bath. Blanch the zucchini and carrots until they are completely tender, a minute or so. Remove them with a skimmer and plunge them into the ice bath.

3. Combine the chicken, egg whites, salt, pepper, and nutmeg in a food processer and puree until smooth. With the machine running, slowly pour in the cream and process until incorporated.

4. Do a quenelle test (see page 28) and adjust the seasoning if necessary, remembering that cooked food served cold requires extra attention.

5. Fold in the blanched vegetables, spinach, roasted red peppers, and herbs. Mix until all ingredients are uniformly incorporated.

6. Line a 1½-quart/1.5-liter terrine mold with plastic wrap and fill it with the mixture. Fold the plastic wrap over the top.

7. Cover with a lid or aluminum foil and cook in the water bath to an internal temperature of 160°F/71°C, 45 to 60 minutes. Remove the terrine from the water bath. When it's cool enough to handle, weight the terrine (see page 30) and refrigerate until thoroughly chilled. Unmold, slice, and serve (see page 30).

YIELD: 15 APPETIZER PORTIONS

Cauliflower, Pea, and Red Pepper Mousse en Terrine

Any vegetable puree can be used to create a vegetable terrine—bright orange carrot or deep red beet or white parsnip—simply by adding the right amount of gelatin to it. The puree can be used to hold any garnish you wish. Or, as here, three differently colored and flavored vegetable purees can be layered for visual appeal. Theoretically, you could add gelatin to a potato puree and fold in chunks of grilled steak for a meat and potatoes terrine, served with a béarnaise sauce. A bit unconventional, perhaps, but a way to use your imagination. Imagination plus a formula: ½ cup/120 milliliters of starch puree and ½ cup/120 milliliters cream into which 1 teaspoon powdered gelatin has been dissolved. This ratio will give you a delicate but sliceable terrine every time. When using nonstarchy vegetables with a high water content—tomatoes, for instance, or the roasted red peppers below—you will need to either cook the water out of them or use more gelatin. You could even make a clear tomato water, but you'd need double the gelatin.

The following recipe is for a tricolor terrine, but the principles hold for all vegetables. For more flavor and a slightly different color, the cauliflower could be roasted rather than steamed, the peppers grilled rather than roasted—another way the formula is useful and versatile. Because vegetables come in various sizes, they may give varying quantities of finished puree, even when measured raw by weight. This means you should plan to have a little more puree than you will actually use.

And one last note: Because all vegetables are fibrous by nature, we instruct here that they all need to be passed through a sieve after being pureed in the food processor; alternatively, you could pass the vegetables through the fine disk of a food mill.

½ head cauliflower (about 12 ounces/ 360 grams), cored and broken into florets

Kosher salt and ground white pepper to taste

1½ cups/200 grams fresh or frozen peas

3 red bell peppers, roasted, peeled, and seeded

6 tablespoons cold water

3 teaspoons powdered gelatin

1½ cups/360 milliliters heavy cream

—

1. Steam the cauliflower until soft, then season with salt and pepper. Puree in a food processor until smooth, then pass it through a fine-mesh sieve. Measure ½ cup/ 120 milliliters into a bowl and set aside.

2. If using fresh peas, blanch them in salted boiling water until tender; if using frozen, just thaw them. Season with salt and pepper. Puree in the food processor until smooth, then pass through a fine-mesh sieve. Measure ½ cup/120 milliliters into a bowl and set aside.

3. Season the roasted peppers with salt. Puree in the food processor until smooth, then pass through a fine-mesh sieve. Transfer the puree to a small saucepan and simmer until thick. Measure ½ cup/120 milliliters into a bowl and set aside.

4. Put 2 tablespoons of cold water in each of three small bowls. Sprinkle 1 teaspoon of powdered gelatin over the water in each bowl. Let sit for 3 to 4 minutes to bloom (that is, absorb the water without forming clumps). Microwave each bowl of bloomed gelatin for 30 seconds or so and stir. Add one bowl of gelatin to each of the vegetable purees and stir well.

5. Whip the heavy cream to stiff peaks. Gently fold one-third of the cream into each of the vegetables. Taste and adjust seasoning as needed.

6. Line a 1½-quart/1.5-liter terrine mold with plastic wrap. Spread the pepper mousse evenly on the bottom, smoothing it with a spatula. Top this with the cauliflower mousse, followed by the pea puree. Smooth the surface, fold the plastic wrap over the top, and refrigerate until thoroughly chilled. Unmold, slice, and serve (see page 30).

YIELD: 12 APPETIZER PORTIONS

Portobello and Roasted Red Pepper Terrine

This is an example of a contemporary terrine rather than a traditional cooked terrine. The ingredients are cooked first, layered in the mold, and bound with a vinaigrette containing gelatin. Slice it fairly thin and serve with arugula salad and grissini bread sticks for a fabulous first course.

10 large portobello mushrooms (2 pounds/1 kilogram), stems removed and gills scraped away

¾ cup/180 milliliters extra virgin olive oil, or as needed

Kosher salt and freshly ground black pepper to taste

2 tablespoons sherry vinegar

1 tablespoon Dijon mustard

½ cup/60 grams fresh basil chiffonade

¼ cup/60 milliliters cold water

1½ teaspoons powdered gelatin

4 red bell peppers (about 2 pounds/ 1 kilogram), roasted, peeled, and seeded

1. Preheat the oven to 375°F/190°C.

2. Toss the mushroom caps with a generous amount of olive oil, then season them with salt and pepper. Lay them on a rimmed baking sheet and roast until soft, 20 to 30 minutes. Allow to cool.

3. In a small bowl, combine the vinegar and mustard and season with salt and pepper. Slowly whisk in ½ cup/120 milliliters olive oil, then stir in the basil.

4. Pour the cold water into a small bowl and sprinkle the gelatin over it. Let it sit for 3 to 4 minutes to bloom (that is, absorb the water without forming clumps). Microwave the bloomed gelatin for 30 seconds or so and stir, then whisk it into the vinaigrette.

5. Line a 1-quart/1-liter terrine mold with plastic wrap. Lay a row of mushroom caps upside down along the bottom of mold, trimming each as needed to fit the mold. Brush them with the vinaigrette.

6. Cut the roasted red peppers into strips to cover the mushrooms, overlapping them end to end. Brush them with the vinaigrette.

7. Repeat as needed to fill the terrine, ending with a layer of mushrooms and more vinaigrette. Fold the plastic wrap over the top, weight the terrine (see page 30), and refrigerate until thoroughly chilled. Unmold, slice, and serve (see page 30).

YIELD: 8 APPETIZER PORTIONS

Two-Potato Terrine

This is an excellent, unusual way to serve potatoes, especially nutrient-dense sweet potatoes: en terrine, held together by the natural starches in the potatoes. It's made ahead, of course, and can be served cold, at room temperature, or warm. Slices can be used to balance meats in a larger charcuterie board—they are delicious with a rich truffle cream or an herby, acidic vinaigrette. Or they can be reheated in the microwave or oven and served warm with salt and pepper, or topped with cheese.

  2 pounds/1 kilogram russet potatoes, peeled

  2 pounds/1 kilogram sweet potatoes, peeled

  2 cups/480 milliliters heavy cream

  Soft unsalted butter as needed

  Kosher salt and freshly ground black pepper to taste

——

1. Preheat the oven to 300°F/150°C.

2. Cut the russet potatoes lengthwise into ¼-inch/6-millimeter slices, and hold them in a bowl of cold water. Do the same with the sweet potatoes, holding them in a separate bowl of cold water. Depending on the size of the potatoes, trim them to about 3 inches/8 centimeters long so that they fit the mold.

3. Heat the cream in a small saucepan to 160°F/71°C—too hot to hold your hand to but before it reaches a simmer.

4. Cut a 12-inch/30-centimeter square of parchment paper. Butter the paper on both sides and butter the inside of a 1½-quart/1.5-liter terrine mold. Line the mold with the buttered paper.

5. Line the bottom of the mold with one-third of the sweet potato slices, putting the pieces next to each other. Season with salt and pepper and pour a little warm cream, about ⅓ cup/80 milliliters, over just to moisten them. Do the same with one-third of the russet potato slices. Repeat until you have six layers, three of each potato.

6. Fold the parchment paper over the top and place an empty terrine mold or other heavy oven-safe object on top to weight it down.

7. Bake until the potatoes are tender when poked with a toothpick, about 1 hour. Let the terrine cool to room temperature, then refrigerate until thoroughly chilled. Unmold, slice, and serve (see page 30).

YIELD: 12 APPETIZER OR SIDE-DISH PORTIONS

TWO-POTATO TERRINE

PART 2

Mousse

Smoked Salmon
Mousse

———

103

Duck Liver Mousse
with Morels

———

104

Pig "Butter"

105

Spuma di Mortadella

———

106

Crema di Lardo

———

107

Chicken Liver Mousse
with Caramelized
Onions

———

108

Cauliflower Mousse

———

110

Chicken Liver
"Butter"

———

111

Mousse is all about texture—a light, airy, soufflé-like consistency that Brian often calls magical. *Mousse* refers to any cooked food that is whipped and lightened with a fat, typically cream (and sometimes egg white). It can be a chocolate pudding that is lightened with whipped cream or a duck liver that is sautéed until it's cooked through, then pureed with seasonings and cream and chilled until it is set. (*Mousseline*, on the other hand, refers to pureed raw food that's set when it is cooked.)

Mousse is a critical asset in the cook's repertoire. It's a great technique in and of itself, creating delectable spreads, but it is also an invaluable way to make use of leftovers. Consider the first recipe in this chapter: It's nothing more than leftover smoked salmon pureed with cream cheese. It's fabulous even though it requires no skill other than adjusting the acidity with lemon. And then there is a duck liver mousse, flavored with onion and reduced wine, which is an impressive preparation on any level. In the contemporary kitchen, we have vegetable mousses as well, such as one made from cauliflower and set with gelatin.

The word *mousse* is from the French word for "foam" (as *spuma* is in Italian), so we also use the term to refer to any food whipped to airy lightness, such as *crema di lardo*, which is entirely fat with no protein whatever.

And that is all there is to it—puree, enrich, season, and set. This technique not only transforms plain food into something ethereal, but often it does so using leftover trim or elevating elemental foods (liver, fat, vegetables) to grandness.

THE BASIC MOUSSE RATIO

As with many fundamental techniques, there is a basic ratio and method. This ratio is by volume rather than by weight, as most other ratios are. But equal parts puree and cream by volume always works, whether the base is cauliflower or duck.

> 2 cups/480 milliliters cooked base puree
>
> 1 tablespoon powdered gelatin
>
> ½ cup/120 milliliters liquid
>
> 2 cups/480 milliliters heavy cream, whipped
>
> 1 tablespoon/15 grams kosher salt (or 1.5% by weight of the puree base, liquid and cream)

For those of you who jones on reducing ratios to their essence, as I do, the ratio tracks thus: 4 parts puree, 4 parts cream, 1 part liquid; seasoned with 1.5 percent salt by weight, and set with 1 tablespoon/ 15 grams powdered gelatin for every 1 quart/1 liter liquid, bloomed and dissolved in that liquid.

Do note that this is not a sliceable mousse. It has a more delicate texture than that, but it can be piped and will hold its shape. If you want to make it sliceable, you'll need to add half again as much gelatin.

The beauty of this formula is that it works for anything you have on hand. Smoked meats such as ham and chicken make fabulous mousses. You need a liquid in which to melt the gelatin, and that liquid can be water, but of course we prefer something more flavorful, so would choose wine or stock or a combination of the two.

Because the pleasure in a mousse is largely about texture, those that use liver call for passing the mixture through a tamis or fine-mesh sieve. This is not strictly necessary, but for a perfect texture, this step removes any fine strands of connective tissue that may not have been cut by the food processor.

The mousse is a great technique to have in your arsenal. The following recipes are a few of the many ways of using mousse, from a traditional duck liver mousse to a simple salmon mousse that requires only three ingredients, to finished preparations, such as lardo and mortadella, that are simply pureed and seasoned.

For step-by-step instructions, see Cauliflower Mousse (page 110).

Smoked Salmon Mousse

This preparation demonstrates how simple and delicious the technique and idea of a mousse is. It calls for just three ingredients: salmon, cream cheese, and lemon juice. Or, more broadly speaking: protein, fat, and seasoning. We'd like to note how valuable cream cheese is. In many ways, it's like a pastry chef's pastry cream, an all-purpose base with many different uses. Here it takes on the flavor, and the seasoning, of salmon—the taste of the fish, the salt it was cured with, and the smoke—and gives it a delightful spreadable texture. This could be a simple morning spread for bagels, or a great dish to set out for hors d'oeuvres. You could make it more elaborate by putting out chopped fresh dill, capers, minced red onion, hard-cooked egg, or any garnish you love on salmon.

8 ounces/225 grams cream cheese

8 ounces/225 grams cold-smoked salmon trimmings

Juice of ½ lemon

1. In a food processor, whip the cream cheese until light. With the machine running, add small chunks of smoked salmon and puree until smooth.

2. Add half of the lemon juice and pulse. Taste for seasoning, and add more lemon juice as needed. (The salmon should provide enough salt, but feel free to add more if you think the mousse needs it.)

3. Press the mousse through a sieve if you would like a very fine, smooth texture, then pipe the mousse onto canapés or transfer to a mold.

YIELD: 8 APPETIZER PORTIONS

Duck Liver Mousse with Morels

There couldn't be a better example than this of how simple the mousse technique is, and how just a little extra effort results in deep deliciousness. It's little more than chopped liver, but enhanced by aromatics, earthy mushrooms, and a wine reduction it becomes an exquisite dish to serve as an hors d'oeuvre or even as a plated appetizer—a quenelle on toast with some spicy greens and a good balsamic vinegar is all you need. Brian puts a spoonful on a crouton with a slice of red grape on top and it's perfect.

Note that the livers are best soaked overnight, but if you're rushed, 2 hours will suffice. This recipe calls for pressing the pureed duck livers through a tamis or a sieve—this has a remarkable impact on the texture and is highly recommended. But feel free to improvise or serve as is.

1 tablespoon/15 grams kosher salt, plus more as needed

2 cups/480 milliliters whole milk

1 pound/450 grams fresh duck livers, veins and connective tissue removed

¼ cup/60 grams unsalted butter plus 1 cup/225 grams unsalted butter, at room temperature

8 ounces/225 grams fresh morels, finely chopped

1 tablespoon minced shallot

Freshly ground black pepper to taste

½ cup/120 milliliters dry sherry

2 tablespoons vegetable oil

½ cup/120 milliliters brandy

1 cup/240 milliliters heavy cream

1. In a bowl, dissolve the salt in the milk. Add the livers, transfer to the refrigerator, and soak for at least 2 hours or overnight.

2. Melt the ¼ cup butter in a sauté pan over medium-high heat and sauté the morels and shallot until their moisture is released. Season with salt and pepper. Deglaze the pan with the sherry and continue cooking until the pan is dry. Set the pan aside to cool to room temperature.

3. Remove the livers from the milk and pat them dry with paper towels (discard the milk).

4. Heat the oil in a sauté pan over high heat and brown the livers on all sides. Deglaze the pan with the brandy, cover, and turn the heat to low. Cook the livers all the way through, about 15 minutes. Set aside to cool to room temperature.

5. Puree the livers and any juices in a food processor, seasoning them with salt and pepper. Add the 1 cup/225 grams soft butter in three stages, scraping down the sides each time, and process until the butter has been incorporated. Pass the liver mixture through a tamis or fine-mesh sieve.

6. Whip the cream to stiff peaks and gently fold it into the liver mixture, along with the morels.

7. Fill a 1-quart/1-liter soufflé dish with the mousse, cover, and refrigerate until thoroughly chilled before serving.

YIELD: 12 APPETIZER PORTIONS

Pig "Butter"

Pig butter is rendered fat from the pig, whether from trim, the belly, or, best, leaf lard, that is whipped into a mousse-like, spreadable texture. It's flavored with onion and is great to have on an hors d'oeuvre table with crusty bread or crackers. It's especially good on grilled bread.

We sometimes refer to whipped preparations like this by the Italian word for "foam," *spuma*. Spuma can refer to other mousse-like spreads mostly made from trim, such as mortadella pieces, which makes a fabulous spuma. Salami ends and fat are sometimes whipped with ricotta or mascarpone to this same texture for similar effects.

2 cups/480 milliliters rendered pork fat (see Note), preferably from leaf lard

½ cup/110 grams finely diced onion

2 tablespoons chopped fresh leafy herbs (such as flat-leaf parsley, chives, and/or chervil)

Kosher salt and freshly ground black pepper to taste

1. Chill the fat in the refrigerator until it is nice and hard. The day before making the pig butter, remove it from the refrigerator and leave it at room temperature overnight. The texture should be that of butter at room temperature: It should retain its shape but be completely spreadable.

2. Melt about 2 tablespoons of the soft fat in a sauté pan over medium heat. Add the onion and cook until it's soft but has no color or browning at all. Allow the onion and fat to cool completely to room temperature.

3. Put the remaining soft pork fat in the bowl of a standing mixer fitted with the whip attachment. Mix at high speed until it looks fluffy and will hold a stiff peak, 5 to 8 minutes. Fold in the cooled onion and fresh herbs by hand and season with salt and pepper. Serve.

YIELD: ABOUT 2 CUPS/480 MILLILITERS

NOTE: To render fat, grind 1 pound/ 450 grams chilled diced leaf lard through a ½-inch/12-millimeter die into a thick-bottomed pot. Add ½ cup/120 milliliters water. Put the pot over medium-high heat and allow the water to come to a simmer as it begins to render the fat. Lower the heat to medium-low and continue to render until the fat is clear, past milky, but before it begins to brown. Strain through a fine-mesh sieve. The rendered fat can also be used as shortening for pastry dough.

Spuma di Mortadella

When Brian and I traveled through Italy for our book *Salumi*, we visited Bologna, mortadella central. Mortadella is that baloney-like forcemeat typically dotted with whole fat and often pistachios. But it tastes different depending on how it's cut. At one restaurant, we were served a "tasting," which comprised cubed mortadella, thinly sliced mortadella, and pureed mortadella, called *spuma* ("foam"). This was culinary invention born not of curiosity but rather clever utilization. Brian often served his own mortadella (see the fantastic recipe in *Charcuterie*) at his restaurant. He was invariably left with the tapered ends, which were too irregularly shaped to slice and sell, so he was always looking for a way to utilize them. After Bologna, he realized he could puree all these ends and serve it as spuma di mortadella.

This is easy to make, and great as an hors d'oeuvres on crostini, with eggs for breakfast, as a filling for pasta, and of course as a standalone item, drizzled with aged balsamic, on a charcuterie board.

8 ounces/225 grams mortadella, cut into ½-inch/1-centimeter dice

¼ cup whole-milk ricotta

½ cup/120 milliliters heavy cream

Freshly grated nutmeg to taste

Freshly ground black pepper to taste

—

1. Pulse the mortadella in a food processor until smooth. The mixture will tighten up a bit.

2. Add the ricotta and pulse a few times. Then, with the machine running, slowly pour in the cream.

3. Season with nutmeg and black pepper and serve.

YIELD: 8 APPETIZER PORTIONS

Crema di Lardo

This is similar to Pig "Butter" (page 105), but the fat is cured rather than cooked, so it's not as light as the fluffy rendered fat. Lardo is cured back fat, which is ground and then pureed with herbs and aromatics to make a delicious, dense spread. The mousse can be used as is or flavored with additional components such as truffle oil or pesto.

8 ounces/225 grams cured lardo

¼ cup whole-milk ricotta

1 tablespoon minced garlic

1½ teaspoons finely chopped fresh rosemary

1½ teaspoons finely chopped fresh flat-leaf parsley

Freshly ground black pepper to taste

1. Grind the lardo through a ⅛-inch/ 3-millimeter die. Transfer to a food processor and add the ricotta and garlic. Puree until smooth.

2. Transfer the fat mixture to a bowl. Fold in the herbs and season with black pepper and serve.

YIELD: 12 APPETIZER PORTIONS

Chicken Liver Mousse with Caramelized Onions

All liver has a mineral-y, or tinny, component owing to its high iron count. Here we use one of the kitchen's most invaluable ingredients, the onion, to balance this.

Brian and I have an ongoing debate about what to call the onion: Is it a vegetable or a seasoning? Brian thinks of the onion as a seasoning, and he's not wrong. The onion is a powerful flavoring device, adding any number of aromatic flavors depending on how you cook it.

For this recipe, we cook almost all the water out of the onion so that its abundant sugars cook and caramelize for the intense sweetness that works so well in a chicken liver mousse.

Serve this mousse with toast.

2 tablespoons/30 grams kosher salt, plus more as needed

2 cups/480 milliliters water

1 pound/450 grams chicken livers, veins and connective tissue removed

¼ cup/60 grams butter plus 1½ cups/340 grams unsalted butter, at room temperature

12 ounces/340 grams thinly sliced sweet onions

Freshly ground black pepper to taste

½ cup/120 milliliters brandy

2 tablespoons finely chopped fresh flat-leaf parsley

2 tablespoons vegetable oil

1. In a bowl, dissolve the salt in the water. Add the livers, transfer to the refrigerator, and soak for at least 2 hours or overnight.

2. Melt the ¼ cup butter in a sauté pan over medium heat. Add the onions, season with salt and pepper, and cover with a tight-fitting lid. Cook until the onions are very soft, 10 to 15 minutes. Remove the lid, turn the heat to medium-high, and cook, stirring, until the liquid cooks off and the onions turn golden brown. Deglaze the pan with half of the brandy and continue to cook until the pan is dry. Remove the pan from the heat and allow to cool. Chop the onions fine and fold in the parsley. The mixture should look spreadable.

3. Remove the livers from the water and pat dry with paper towels. Heat the oil in a sauté pan over high heat and sear the livers for about a minute per side. Reduce the heat to low, cover the pan, and cook until the livers are firm, 3 to 5 minutes. Deglaze with the remaining brandy, cook to reduce the juices, then set aside to cool to room temperature.

4. Puree the livers in a food processor until smooth. Add the 1½ cups/340 grams soft butter in three stages, scraping down the sides each time, and process until the butter has been incorporated. Pass the liver mixture through a tamis or fine-mesh sieve.

5. Fill a 1-quart/1-liter soufflé dish with the mousse, cover, and refrigerate for 1 hour.

6. Spread the firm top with the onion mixture. Cover and refrigerate overnight.

7. Remove from the fridge 1 hour before serving to allow the mixture to soften.

YIELD: 12 APPETIZER PORTIONS

Cauliflower Mousse

Cauliflower mousse is a great preparation in its own right, but it is also a great formula, or ratio, for turning a vegetable puree into a gorgeously textured mousse. Use 2 cups/480 milliliters puree, 2 cups/480 milliliters heavy cream, and 1 tablespoon powdered gelatin. This results in a delicate mousse, one that is not quite sliceable, but one that you can pipe from a pastry bag or even a plastic zip-top bag with a corner cut off. Brian likes to create canapés on spoons and garnish with osetra caviar or a *pluche* of chervil. But you could also pipe this mousse on top of cucumber disks, fill hollowed-out baby zucchini or radishes with it, and so on. And of course, you could also roast the cauliflower (whole at 425°F/218°C for 1 hour, basting midway through with 6 tablespoons/90 grams butter) rather than boil it.

1 head cauliflower, cored and broken into florets

Kosher salt and freshly ground black pepper to taste

½ cup/120 milliliters vegetable stock

1 tablespoon powdered gelatin

2 cups/480 milliliters heavy cream

1. Bring a large pot of well-salted water to a boil, add the cauliflower, and cook until tender, about 5 minutes. Chill under cold running water.

2. Drain the cauliflower well and puree with salt and pepper in a food processor or food mill until very smooth. Pass the mousse through a tamis or fine-mesh sieve. Measure out 2 cups/480 milliliters of puree for the mousse base.

3. Pour the stock into a small saucepan and sprinkle the gelatin over it. Let it sit for 3 to 4 minutes to bloom (that is, absorb the stock without forming clumps). Warm over medium-low heat to dissolve the gelatin. Beat the aspic into the cauliflower.

4. Whip the cream to stiff peaks and gently fold into the cauliflower base. Season with salt and pepper and serve.

YIELD: 24 CANAPÉ PORTIONS

Chicken Liver "Butter"

Chicken liver can be almost sweet; this, plus the consistency and lightness and the way it is used as a spread, is why we use the term *butter* to distinguish this preparation from other pâtés and mousses. It is similar to the Chicken Liver Terrine (page 59), but because of the added butter, it's got a light, mousse-like texture and can be spread or piped—perfect for passed canapés. It can also be put in a mold and chilled, then turned out and sliced. In either case, it should be tempered (allowed to warm up a bit) at room temperature or the butter will be too hard. It goes very well with hard-cooked egg as a garnish, as well as with capers and minced red onion.

2 tablespoons/30 grams kosher salt, plus more as needed

2 cups/480 milliliters water

1 pound/450 grams chicken livers, veins and connective tissue removed

Freshly ground black pepper to taste

2 tablespoons vegetable oil

½ cup/110 grams finely sliced onion

¼ cup/60 milliliters brandy

1 pound/450 grams unsalted butter, at room temperature

1. In a bowl, dissolve the salt in the water. Add the livers, transfer to the refrigerator, and soak for at least 4 hours or overnight. Remove the livers from the water and pat dry with paper towels. Season with salt and pepper.

2. Heat the oil on a sauté pan over medium-high heat and sear the livers on both sides, about a minute per side. Add the onion and cook until the livers are cooked through and the onion is soft, a couple more minutes. Add the brandy and reduce until the liquid is a syrup consistency. Set aside to cool to room temperature.

3. Puree the liver mixture in a food processor until smooth. Add the soft butter in three stages, scraping down the sides each time, and process until the puree is light in color and the butter has been incorporated.

4. Pass the liver through a tamis or fine-mesh strainer. Transfer to a mold lined with plastic wrap for slicing or to small soufflé cups for a potted presentation. Cover and chill overnight before serving.

YIELD: 8 APPETIZER PORTIONS

Foie Gras

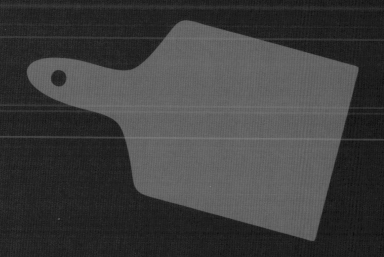

÷→⇢→←→←⇠←÷

Thinking about cooking foie gras is almost as much fun as actually cooking it because it's such an unusual product. But of course, it is much more fun to eat foie gras than to simply think about eating foie gras because the pleasure is so ethereal. For such a luxury, this is as it should be.

If you do not know how special foie gras is, you haven't had it—or you haven't had it properly prepared. Foie gras is very easy to prepare badly. Cut too thin and sautéed, it overcooks and becomes a diminutive shred of itself, with an unpleasant flavor and texture. If it has been cooked in a terrine but is served skimpily and with a rim of gray around it, it has oxidized and the flavor will be off, and of course the texture will have been compromised as well. The proper texture of foie gras is unusual—and one of its great pleasures.

Happily, foie gras is just as easy to prepare well. When you present a properly sautéed medallion of foie gras that has been cut at least ¾ inch/2 centimeters thick and has been scored, sautéed rare to medium-rare, and given a beautiful crust with a sprinkling of Maldon salt, you are serving an unparalleled delicacy.

By far the best way to prepare and serve and eat foie gras is lightly cooked and served cold in the form of a pâté. Here the glory of the foie gras—its mild, sweet flavor and rich, butter-like texture—is at its peak. Indeed, it seems to have been the preferred way of preparing foie gras in one of its homelands, France. (Israel is also famed for its foie gras. Foie gras's origins date to the ancient Egyptians.) So much so that when French food began to migrate to the United States in the 1950s and 1960s, the term *pâté* became almost exclusively associated with foie gras. While pâtés can certainly be made of foie gras, few are. The majority of pâtés need no liver of any kind—though, of course, many owe their rich taste and smooth texture to the judicious use of pork or calf or chicken liver.

Foie is the French word for liver, and *gras* means fat. The term originally referred to the fattened liver of the goose, but foie gras from the Muscovy duck (or the Mulard, a hybrid of Muscovy and Pekin ducks) accounts for most of the foie gras served in the United States. But calling it liver—or thinking of it as liver or tasting like liver—does it a disservice, at least for those who know only ordinary liver, because *foie gras is not like ordinary liver at all*. It doesn't have that strong iron flavor and spongy texture that chicken and calf liver has. Because of its extraordinary fat content, it is more like a savory butter than a meat.

Much misunderstanding surrounds the breeding and raising of ducks for their liver because they are fed a substantial diet via a feeding tube slipped down the throat. In the early 2000s, American farms that raised ducks for foie gras, and especially chefs who served foie gras, were subject to much protest (one chef's home was vandalized and his family threatened) for perceived cruelty to animals.

Having visited foie gras farms and seen the ducks being fed and raised, we can only say that we wish all animals raised for our food could be treated with such care. The ducks had plenty of pasture to roam. When in the fattening stages, called *gavage*, they waddled eagerly to the person feeding them. Indeed, the fattened liver is so delicate a product that only a well-tended and stress-free duck could grow this valuable food. (The breast, called *magret*, is as rich and thick and juicy as a medium-rare strip steak. The legs are typically used for confit; see pages 159 to 179.)

California banned foie gras from being sold in 2004, and a judge ruled in 2017 that the ban could be reinstated. This will and should be resisted. Frankly, both Brian and I believe that anyone who is in favor of the ban but is not also in favor of a ban on all animals being raised for their meat is misinformed at best. Ducks raised for foie gras, at least on good farms, are among the best-treated animals anywhere. Protest the raising of animals for meat, by all means, but don't try to single out and outlaw foie gras for its supposed cruelty.

The issue doesn't generate much media anymore. Perhaps the foie gras protestors have set their sights elsewhere (there are, in fact, problems in our food system of a much greater magnitude, such as the billions of commodity animals on so-called factory farms, that could benefit from their attention). For whatever reason, the brouhaha has happily died down, and now cooks can get back to cooking.

And the cooking of foie gras is fun indeed.

Here we present a standard of preparation—a fundamental ratio and technique—and then offer examples of the primary ways foie gras can be used in the charcutier's kitchen. The recipe we begin with is the very special form of this pâté called a *foie gras au torchon*—French for "foie gras in a dishtowel"—along with the basic seasoning ratio and fundamental principles of working with foie gras that is to be served cold. The second recipe is virtually the same thing, only cooked in a terrine mold. We also offer a foie gras mousse, a whipped preparation that's lighter than a pâté, and we have a terrine in which chunks of foie gras serve as an enriching garnish in a conventional meat-based terrine. And finally, there is a more contemporary preparation that pairs foie gras with one of its great partners, mango (though you could also use peach or sweet-tart apple, or even tart Michigan cherries).

THE FOIE GRAS AU TORCHON

I learned this preparation in 1997 while working with Thomas Keller at his restaurant the French Laundry in Yountville, California. It was he who taught me the fundamentals of serving foie gras. Every afternoon, at around three o'clock, Keller portioned the foie gras that would be sautéed. He cut each piece with his long slicing knife (I never saw him use a chef's knife), seeming to take great pleasure with each stroke through the soft, clay-like lobe. Each medallion was ½ to ¾ inch/15 to 20 millimeters thick. "You have to cut it this thick in order to get a good sear on the outside and the right texture inside. A lot of chefs, because it's such an expensive ingredient, cut the foie gras too thin. When it's too thin you can't get a good sear without overcooking the inside. The inside should be molten."

Likewise, with the foie gras au torchon, he would serve a thick slice, nearly as thick as a hockey puck, saying, "You have to serve these expensive ingredients in abundance, so that people recognize what the fuss is all about, why it's worth the cost. Too often chefs skimp on amounts and you can't fully appreciate why these things are so good. It's the same with caviar, and truffles. You almost have to overdo it."

Back in the 1980s, having been a chef for a decade, Keller had never worked with foie gras, even though he had cooked under some of the best French chefs in the country. This is because there was no one producing foie gras in America at the time, and it couldn't be imported raw (only in the form of pâté).* So it wasn't until he was able to travel to France and cook in kitchens there that he learned how to work with foie gras. And that is where he learned the seasoning ratio that he still uses at his restaurants. Our ratio is identical except for the amount of salt—we use 2 percent rather than 1 percent.

Pink salt, sodium nitrite, keeps the color appealingly bright; in France they use something called *sel rose* or some form of potassium nitrate. Both are forms of naturally occurring nitrogen attached to a form of salt and should not be considered a chemical additive but rather a naturally occurring one (we get most of our nitrates, which are arguably beneficial to our health, from green vegetables, which pick it up from the soil); that said, it's not required for safety as it is in many smoked and dry-cured meats, so it can be considered optional, if you wish.

The basic method for foie gras pâtés is the same. The foie gras is carefully cleaned of the network of veins that run through it. This is probably the most time-consuming part of the process. The more veins and blood that you can get out of the foie gras, the better. The cook should be careful and gentle, but not too concerned with tearing the foie gras apart as it will all eventually be compacted together in the end.

The next step is to soak it overnight in milk in order to leach any remaining blood from the foie gras. Some argue that this is an unnecessary step, but it certainly doesn't hurt; do it if you have the time.

---

* It wouldn't be until the late 1970s or early 1980s that chef Jean-Louis Palladin, originally from Gascony in southwestern France, the country's foie gras capital, figured out how to get fresh foie gras into his restaurant at the Watergate Hotel in Washington, DC. Palladin thus made it possible for all chefs to begin serving foie gras, and for companies such as Hudson Valley Foie Gras to begin producing it.

Next, season the foie gras. Because foie gras comes in varying weights, you must measure the seasonings relative to whatever weight you are working with. You'll need a scale that measures in tenths of a gram.

The foie gras is marinated overnight, after which it can be cooked. Here, the torchon is rolled in cheesecloth and briefly poached in barely simmering water, so briefly that the inside really doesn't even get hot, just warm enough to soften it. If you are cooking it in a terrine (see page 22), you pack it in a terrine and cook it in a water bath—again, just barely—to cooler than rare.

The foie gras is then compacted again—either by rerolling as with the torchon, or by pressing it in its terrine mold. Once completely chilled, it's ready to be sliced. (Foie gras can remain in the fridge for up to 7 days, and it can be well wrapped and frozen for up to a month.) As a rule, pâté de foie gras should be sliced between ½ and ¾ inch/15 to 20 millimeters thick.

Pâté de foie gras is best served simply. All you really need is some toasted brioche and, ideally, something sweet and tart to offset the richness. This can be as simple as a *brunoise* of Granny Smith apple. At the French Laundry, among the many garnishes Keller used were pickled Bing cherries. Brian likes his Great Lakes tart cherries or mango or any pickled fruit. The pâté is very rich and very soft, so as long as you have something a little crunchy and something tart (and, if you wish, a neutral ingredient for color—some leaves of mâche, for instance), anything goes. And it's often served with an expensive sweet wine, such as a Sauternes, and this is grand, but foie gras is also excellent with a crisp Champagne or other dry bubbly white wine.

Foie Gras au Torchon

Because one often works with differing sizes and amounts of foie gras, a general seasoning ratio is essential. With the ratio, you can work with any amount of foie gras you happen to have on hand.

FOR EVERY 100 GRAMS OF FOIE GRAS:

2 grams kosher salt (2%)

0.1 grams finely ground white or black pepper (0.1%)

0.2 grams sugar (0.2%)

0.25 grams pink curing salt (0.25%)

1 gram brandy or Sauternes, optional (1%)

Day One

1. Pull apart the foie gras lobes and remove as many veins as possible. Remove any sinew or membranes from the outside of the foie. If there are any bruised parts, cut them away and discard. Working from the bottom of the lobes, butterfly them and locate the primary vein in the center of each. Slice through the lobe to the vein, following its path and pulling the foie apart to see the vein clearly. (Don't worry if you mangle the foie—better to get the veins out.)

2 Weigh the foie gras and record the weight (whole foie gras typically weigh a little more than a pound, or around 500 grams).

3. Put the foie gras in a baking dish and cover with milk. (This, we believe, helps leach out some of the blood exposed by the cleaning; if you wish to omit this step, that's up to you.) Press plastic wrap down onto the surface of the liquid. Refrigerate overnight or for up to 2 days.

Day Two

1. Drain and rinse the foie gras (discard the milk); pat dry. Calculate the amounts of seasonings by weight, and measure them out. To do this, multiply the percentage of each by the weight of the foie gras. (For example: If the foie gras weighs 800 grams: $800 \times 0.02 =$ 16 grams kosher salt; $800 \times 0.001 = 0.8$ grams pepper; $800 \times 0.002 = 1.6$ grams sugar; $800 \times 0.0025 = 2$ grams pink salt; $800 \times 0.01 = 8$ grams brandy.)

2. Mix the seasonings well and sprinkle evenly over the foie gras. Press the foie into a container in an even layer ¾ to 1 inch/2 to 2.5 centimeters thick. Sprinkle it with the alcohol, if using, massaging the seasonings over the foie gras. Press a piece of plastic directly against the foie gras so it is in contact with as little air as possible. Refrigerate for 12 to 24 hours.

RECIPE CONTINUES ↪

Day Three

1. Remove the foie from the container and let it rest for an hour or two at room temperature to make it easier to work with. Place it on a piece of parchment paper (best) or plastic wrap (will suffice) in the form of a loaf about 6 by 3 inches/15 by 8 centimeters. Roll the foie into a log, twisting and squeezing the ends of the parchment paper or plastic to help compact it.

2. Unwrap the foie, discard the paper or plastic, and transfer the log to a piece of cheesecloth about 1 by 2 feet/30 by 60 centimeters. Place the foie on the short end of the cheesecloth. Begin to roll it to force the foie into a compact log again.

3. Using butcher's twine, loop a length of string around your index finger. With the same hand, hold one end of the cheesecloth tightly and wind the string around the end of the foie. Continue wrapping the string about ¼ inch/6 millimeters into the foie gras; by winding the string around the end, you will compress the foie gras into an increasingly tight roll. When the foie is as compressed as possible, tie it off. Repeat the procedure on the other end. Tie a few ties along its girth for extra support.

4. Fill a wide pot with enough water (or, if you have it, veal or chicken stock) to submerge the foie gras; bring it to a simmer. Prepare an ice bath. Place the torchon in the gently simmering liquid for 90 seconds. Immediately transfer the torchon to the ice bath to cool for 5 to 10 minutes.

5. The foie will be loose in the cloth. Make it compact again by compressing it in a second cloth (leaving the first one on). Roll it as tightly as possible. Twist and tie the ends of the towel with a string and hang the torchon from a shelf in the refrigerator overnight.

Day Four

Unwrap the foie gras, slice, and serve—or, for an especially elegant appearance worthy of, say, the French Laundry, slice, cut with a ring mold to remove ragged edges, and serve with an appropriate garnish as noted above.

YIELD: 2 OUNCES/60 GRAMS PER SERVING

VARIATION:
Salt-Cured Foie Gras au Torchon

Brian and I have a great affection for Thomas Keller, not only as a chef but as a person. His method of poaching the torchon for 90 seconds softens the exterior but does not cook the center, allowing him to compact the foie gras for a perfect appearance. Brian loves this method but he also loves to salt-cure the foie gras, which eliminates the risk of overcooking and thus is pretty much foolproof.

Follow the method for the Foie Gras au Torchon through the wrapping of the foie gras in cheesecloth. But instead of poaching the foie gras, fill a dish with kosher salt. Place the foie gras on the salt and cover it completely with more salt. Refrigerate for 3 days. Remove the foie gras from the salt. Remove the cheesecloth, slice, and serve.

Foie Gras en Terrine with Sauternes

This is a classic preparation and uses roughly two whole foie gras. Use this recipe if you are serving 15 to 20 people at a celebratory dinner. (If you want to prepare less foie gras, see the following recipe, which uses smaller molds.)

This is the same pâté as in the Foie Gras au Torchon (page 119). The cooking method is different; here we use a water bath, so the foie gras is ever so slightly more cooked. It is weighted, too, so that it is compressed rather than being rolled, and we add a little more salt. But the taste and texture should be more or less the same. See the torchon notes about serving and garnish (page 118).

3 pounds/1350 grams grade A foie gras

2 cups/480 milliliters milk, as needed

3 tablespoons/45 grams kosher salt

1 tablespoon ground white pepper

1 tablespoon sugar

½ teaspoon pink curing salt, optional (but recommended for color)

1½ cups/360 milliliters Sauternes

¾ cup/180 milliliters brandy

1. Pull apart the foie gras lobes and remove as many veins as possible. Remove any sinew or membranes from the outside of the foie. If there are any bruised parts, cut them away and discard. Working from the bottom of the lobes, butterfly them and locate the primary vein in the center of each. Slice through the lobe to the vein, following its path and pulling the foie apart to see the vein clearly. (Don't worry if you mangle the foie—better to get the veins out.)

2. Put the foie gras in a baking dish and cover with milk. (This, we believe, helps leach out some of the blood exposed by the cleaning; if you wish to omit this step, that's up to you.) Press plastic wrap down onto the surface of the liquid. Refrigerate overnight or for up to 2 days. Drain and rinse the foie gras (discard the milk); pat dry and put the foie gras in a zip-top plastic bag.

3. Mix the seasonings well and sprinkle over the foie gras. Pour the alcohol over the foie and massage the marinade over the foie gras. Seal and refrigerate the foie gras for 12 to 24 hours.

4. Allow the foie gras to come to room temperature for at least 2 hours or up to 6 hours.

5. Prepare a water bath in a 300°F/150°C oven (see page 30).

RECIPE CONTINUES ↪

6. Line a 1½-quart/1.5-liter terrine mold with plastic wrap. Press the foie gras into the mold tightly, ensuring there are no air gaps. Fold the plastic wrap over the top.

7. Cover with a lid or aluminum foil and cook in the water bath to an internal temperature of 118°F/48°C, 30 to 40 minutes. Remove the terrine from the water bath and drain off the excess rendered fat (reserve it to sauté diced brioche for elegant croutons, for instance). When it's cool enough to handle, weight the terrine (see page 30) and refrigerate until thoroughly chilled. Unmold, slice, and serve (see page 30).

YIELD: 15 TO 20 APPETIZER PORTIONS

FOIE GRAS EN TERRINE WITH SAUTERNES
(PAGE 121), SPRINKLED WITH SEA SALT
AND SERVED WITH DRIED TART CHERRY
MARMALADE (PAGE 231)

Foie Gras en Terrine in Smaller Molds

Say you don't want to serve 3 pounds of foie gras. Say you have only half a foie gras. Say you are a chef and you have 12 ounces/360 grams of ends left after cutting foie gras to be sautéed. Or say you have only a 6-by-3-inch/15-by-8-centimeter terrine mold, or several smaller molds that might serve one, two, or four people. Or say that you are an ambitious home cook and want to splurge on a foie gras for you and your gourmand friends; you want to sauté some of the foie gras to serve hot and then serve the rest of it as a pâté de foie gras.

That's when the seasoning ratio comes in handy. To gauge the amount of foie gras you'll need to fill a given terrine mold, use water: We've found that if you have a terrine mold that holds 10 ounces/280 grams of water, you will need 10 ounces/280 grams of foie gras to fill it.

Follow the seasoning ratio used for the Foie Gras au Torchon (page 119), and the general method for the Foie Gras en Terrine (page 121), with whatever size mold you would like to use. (If you don't have the right size molds for the amount of foie gras you need to cook, you can make small torchons. In this case, follow the torchon recipe and technique, page 119.)

If the scraps of foie gras you want to use don't hold together or are not sufficiently elegant, after the pâté has been cooked and cooled, you can press it through a tamis and pipe it into individual ramekins.

FOR EVERY 100 GRAMS FOIE GRAS:

2 grams kosher salt (2%)

0.1 grams finely ground white or black pepper (0.1%)

0.2 grams sugar (0.2%)

0.25 grams pink curing salt (0.25%)

1 gram brandy or Sauternes, optional (1%)

1. If using a whole foie gras, pull apart the lobes and remove as many veins as possible. Remove any sinew or membranes from the outside of the foie. If there are any bruised parts, cut them away and discard. Working from the bottom of the lobes, butterfly them and locate the primary vein in the center of each. Slice through the lobe to the vein, following its path and pulling the foie apart to see the vein clearly. (Don't worry if you mangle the foie—better to get the veins out.)

2. Put your terrine mold on a scale. Hit the tare, or zero, button. Fill the mold with water. Record the weight of the water. Repeat, as necessary, if you are using multiple small molds.

3. Weigh out the same amount of cleaned foie gras.

4. Put the foie gras in a baking dish and cover with milk. (This, we believe, helps leach out some of the blood exposed by the cleaning; if you wish to omit this step, that's up to you.) Press plastic wrap down onto the surface of the liquid. Refrigerate overnight or for up to 2 days. Drain and rinse the foie gras (discard the milk); pat dry.

5. Calculate the amounts of seasonings by weight, and measure them out. Mix the seasonings well and sprinkle evenly over the foie gras. Calculate and weigh out the alcohol, if using, and sprinkle it over the foie, massaging the seasonings over the foie gras. Press a piece of plastic wrap directly against the foie gras so it is in contact with as little air as possible. Refrigerate for 12 to 24 hours.

6. Allow the foie gras to come to room temperature for at least 2 hours or up to 6 hours.

7. Prepare a water bath in a 300°F/150°C oven (see page 29).

8. Line your terrine mold(s) with plastic wrap. Press the foie gras into each mold tightly, ensuring there are no air gaps. Fold the plastic wrap over the top.

9. Cover with a lid or aluminum foil and cook in the water bath to an internal temperature of 115°F/46°C, 20 to 30 minutes, depending on the size of your mold(s). Remove the terrine from the water bath and drain off the excess rendered fat (reserve it to sauté diced brioche for elegant croutons, for instance). When it's cool enough to handle, weight the terrine (see page 30) and refrigerate until thoroughly chilled. Unmold, slice, and serve (see page 30).

YIELD: 2 OUNCES/60 GRAMS PER SERVING

FOIE GRAS MOUSSE

Foie Gras Mousse

When Brian hosted a gang of certified master chefs at the school where he teaches charcuterie, Schoolcraft College in Livonia, Michigan, outside Detroit, he served them this mousse. The visiting chefs, no strangers to foie gras, were goggle-eyed.

This method takes advantage of the great flavor of seared foie gras, the browned exterior, and the more gently cooked interior. It adds the aromatic sweetness of cooked garlic and shallot and the addition of butter—yes, butter!—to the finished puree. You don't make experienced chefs goggle-eyed by holding back, do you?

This is so good that Brian recommends serving it simply with toasted brioche points (and perhaps a perfect, crisp Champagne or blanc de blancs).

1½ pounds/680 grams grade B foie gras

1 quart/1 liter whole milk

5 tablespoons/75 grams kosher salt

1 teaspoon ground white pepper

¼ cup/60 milliliters Sauternes

¼ cup/60 milliliters brandy

¾ cup/170 grams unsalted butter

¼ cup minced shallot

3 tablespoons minced garlic

1 cup/240 milliliters heavy cream

Day One

1. Pull apart the foie gras lobes and remove as many veins as possible. Remove any sinew or membranes from the outside of the foie. If there are any bruised parts, cut them away and discard. Working from the bottom of the lobes, butterfly them and locate the primary vein in the center of each. Slice through the lobe to the vein, following its path and pulling the foie apart to see the vein clearly. (Don't worry if you mangle the foie—better to get the veins out.) Put the foie gras in a zip-top plastic bag.

2. Add the milk and 4 tablespoons/ 60 grams of the salt to the bag, press out the air, and seal it so that the milk and salt are in contact with the foie gras. Refrigerate for 12 to 24 hours.

Day Two

1. Drain and rinse the foie gras (discard the milk); pat dry. Allow the foie gras to come to room temperature for at least 2 hours or up to 6 hours.

2. Combine the remaining 1 tablespoon/ 15 grams kosher salt, the white pepper, and alcohol in a fresh zip-top plastic bag. Add the foie gras, press out the air, and seal it. Marinate in the refrigerator for 12 to 24 hours.

RECIPE CONTINUES ↷

Day Three

1. Remove the liver from the bag and pat dry with paper towels. Cut it into 1-inch/2.5-centimeter dice. Return it to the bag, seal, and refrigerate.

2. Melt the butter in a sauté pan over medium-high heat. Sauté the shallot and garlic just until tender and without browning them. When they are tender and translucent, turn the heat to high and add the diced foie gras and cook, stirring continuously, until the foie gras dice are just cooked through, 3 to 4 minutes.

3. Transfer the contents of the pan to a plate and allow to cool to room temperature.

4. Puree the mixture in a food processor until smooth. Pass the puree through a fine-mesh sieve into a metal bowl set in an ice bath. Stir the puree constantly until it starts to thicken.

5. Whip the cream to soft peaks and gently fold it into the foie gras. Taste and adjust the seasoning.

6. Fill 6 small (½-cup/120-milliliter) ramekins or soufflé dishes with the foie gras mousse, cover with plastic wrap, and refrigerate.

7. Remove the ramekins from the refrigerator 30 to 60 minutes before you intend to serve them.

YIELD: 24 APPETIZER PORTIONS

Duck and Foie Gras en Terrine

This is a basic duck terrine, like the master recipe (page 36), with the same enrichments and aromatics but different interior garnishes—including foie gras. Of course, some people will get a nice chunk of that foie gras, and some won't. If you're not lucky and don't get a chunk of foie—well, that's the way the pâté slices.

12 ounces/340 grams lean duck leg and thigh meat, cut into 1-inch/2.5-centimeter dice

10 ounces/280 grams pork back fat, cut into 1-inch/2.5-centimeter dice

5 ounces/140 grams slab bacon, cut into 1-inch/2.5-centimeter dice

2 teaspoons/10 grams kosher salt, plus more as needed

1 teaspoon ground white pepper

1 teaspoon All-Purpose Spice Mix for Meat Pâtés (page 33)

½ teaspoon pink curing salt, optional (but recommended)

12 ounces/340 grams foie gras, cut into 1-inch/2.5-centimeter dice

2 (4- to 5-ounce/110- to 140-gram) boneless, skinless duck breasts

1 tablespoon minced shallot

½ cup/120 milliliters ruby port

¼ cup/60 milliliters brandy

1 large egg

¾ cup/180 milliliters heavy cream

5 ounces/140 grams smoked beef tongue, cut into ¼-inch/6-millimeter dice

1. Prepare a water bath in a 300°F/150°C oven (see page 29).

2. In a bowl, toss the diced duck leg meat, back fat, and bacon with the kosher salt, pepper, pâté spice, and pink salt (if using). Cover with plastic wrap and refrigerate overnight.

3. In a dry sauté pan, sear the diced foie gras over high heat on all sides, leaving the centers raw. Transfer to a plate, cover, and refrigerate.

4. Season the duck breasts with salt. Return the pan to high heat. In the residual foie gras fat left in the pan, sear the duck breasts on all sides, leaving the centers raw. Transfer to a plate, cover, and refrigerate.

5. Drain the excess fat from the pan, reduce the heat to medium, and sauté the shallot until translucent but not browned. Deglaze the pan with the port and brandy, reduce the liquid to a syrup, then set the pan aside to cool.

6. Grind the chilled duck leg meat, back fat, and bacon through a ⅛-inch/3-millimeter die into a metal bowl set in an ice bath. Transfer the ground meat to a chilled food processor bowl, add the egg and cooled reduction, and puree until smooth. Return the mixture to the bowl, still in its ice bath, and slowly fold in the cream.

RECIPE CONTINUES ↪

7. Do a quenelle test (see page 28) and adjust the seasoning if necessary, remembering that cooked food served cold requires extra attention.

8. Fold in the seared foie gras and smoked tongue.

9. Line a 1½-quart/1.5-liter terrine mold with plastic wrap. Fill the mold halfway with the pureed meat, making sure to press it well into the corners. Lay the duck breasts in a single layer, pressing them down into the puree, then cover with the remaining puree. Fold the plastic wrap over the top.

10. Cover with a lid or aluminum foil and cook it in the water bath to an internal temperature of 135°F/57°C, 45 to 60 minutes. Remove the terrine from the water bath. When it's cool enough to handle, weight the terrine (see page 30) and refrigerate until thoroughly chilled. Unmold, slice, and serve (see page 30).

YIELD: 15 APPETIZER PORTIONS

Mango and Foie Gras en Terrine

When Jean-Georges Vongerichten opened a restaurant in Thailand in 1980, he may have been the first western chef to pair foie gras with mango (apples, what he normally paired with foie gras, were hard to come by there—he had to improvise). By the mid-1990s, my friend Michael Symon, then chef of Lola in Cleveland's Tremont district, gave me a taste of sautéed foie gras with mango, grinning about what an amazing pair the two were. Since then I've loved combining the tart, sweet tropical fruit with the rich, fatty duck liver. Brian developed this elegant terrine to celebrate the pairing. Mango is perfect, but tart apples would work well, too. The foie is quickly sautéed for flavor, the terrine is layered, then it cooks in a water bath to a below-rare temperature. You need little more than a drizzle of reduced balsamic vinegar or *crema di balsamico* to finish the dish.

 1¼ pounds/600 grams grade B foie gras

 1 teaspoon/5 grams kosher salt

 ¼ teaspoon ground white pepper

 ¼ cup/60 milliliters brandy

 2 ripe mangos, pitted, peeled, and cut lengthwise into ¼-inch/6-millimeter slices

———

1. Separate the lobes of the foie gras and remove any exposed veins or fat. Dip a sharp, thin-bladed slicing knife in hot water and cut the liver lengthwise into 1-inch/2.5-centimeter slabs. At this point clean any remaining veins, fat, or blood spots, while keeping the slabs whole.

2. Put the foie gras in a baking dish or zip-top plastic bag. Season with the salt and pepper, sprinkle with the brandy, cover, and marinate in the refrigerator for at least 2 hours or overnight.

3. Prepare a water bath in a 300°F/150°C oven (see page 29).

4. In a sauté pan, sear both sides of the foie gras slabs over medium heat, making sure the centers are still raw. Transfer to a plate. In the same pan, cook the mango just to soften it, then transfer to another plate (try drizzling the leftover fat on popcorn).

5. Line a 2-cup/480-milliliter mold with plastic wrap. Layer the foie gras and mango alternately until the mold is full. Fold the plastic wrap over the top.

6. Cover with a lid or aluminum foil and cook in the water bath to an internal temperature of 118°F/48°C, 20 to 30 minutes. Remove the terrine from the water bath and drain some of the excess rendered fat. When it's cool enough to handle, weight the terrine (see page 30) and refrigerate until thoroughly chilled. Unmold, slice, and serve (see page 30).

YIELD: 8 APPETIZER PORTIONS

Crust

Combining pâté with a crust does not add a single element to the pâté, it adds a fleet of them: When you give the pâté a rich, browned, crisp, flaky outer crust, you add dimensions in texture, color, and flavor.

A crust can be as simple as a basic dough shaped in a tart pan and filled with a pâté to be cooked. Or it can be a carefully made dough, rolled thin, cut precisely, fitted into a mold, filled with pâté you've studded with bright garnish, then enclosed in the dough, which is then brushed with egg wash and baked, resulting in the magisterial pâté en croûte, a slice of which can be as exciting to behold as it is to savor.

Dough has long been used to add some bulk to a meal and serve leftovers in an appealing way; covering leftover chicken and gravy with a crust gives you a rustic pot pie, just as wrapping pâté forcemeat in dough can give you a free-form meat pie. A crust also made meat portable—you could take a cold meat pie to work, like the English pasty. Paul Bocuse famously covered truffled consommé with puff pastry, which baked up into a golden-brown dome of shatteringly flaky crust

that, when broken with a spoon, released a cloud of heady truffle aroma into the air. It was that crust, I would argue, and not the consommé itself, that made this dish iconic.

The pâté en croûte is perhaps the most difficult of the preparations in this book, the craft of the charcutier brought to its farthest reaches. The pâté en croûte is so revered in its homeland, France, that each year the town of Tain-l'Hermitage, south of Lyon, holds the *Championnat du Monde de Pâté-Croûte*, in which chefs from all over the world compete for ten final spots to prepare meat pies for a panel of chef-judges. (The 2017 competition was won by a Japanese chef, proving that the pâté en croûte is indeed a craft appreciated worldwide.) The pâté en croûte is difficult, but it is so extraordinary that it should never be allowed to disappear from modern cooking. Thus we have gone to some effort to attempt to convey all the elements and their successful creation.

But pâté en croûte can also be as simple as a meat pie, made either in a pie plate, free-form, or, simplest of all, a log of pâté rolled in a sheet of dough and baked. We call the latter two "raised" pies, a term that seems to have originated in England to refer to free-form pies that are about twice as tall as a pie plate. We also use the term for pâté rolled in dough, baked, and sliced to serve.

The recipes in this chapter describe the various ways to give pâté a crisp, browned crust, and to appreciate generally how a simple crust can transform a meat or vegetable puree. We begin with the doughs, and then move on to the pâté en croûte method, which provides good lessons for crusted pâtés, and the regal pâté en croûte itself. We give only one pâté en croûte recipe here, but you can substitute any of the pâtés in this book for the rabbit pâté here. The principles remain the same no matter what kind of pâté you use.

DOUGH BASICS

We offer three basic dough recipes, each with a slightly different taste and texture. The main factor distinguishing them is their fat content (see page 139). The Decker Dough (page 141), named for the chef who developed it, is more than 30 percent fat. We especially love to use this dough for the pâté en croûte for its flavor and texture, and for how easy it is to work with in terms of lining the mold.

The dough for a pâté en croute—indeed, for most crust preparations—should be cold but pliable. If the fat is too hard, it will be too difficult to roll out and will stress the dough. So it's best to let a chilled dough rest, uncovered, for 30 minutes before rolling it out.

When you do roll it, you want to make it as thin as possible while still being able to lift it into the mold. It will expand with the cooking, and you don't want the crust to be doughy; rather, you want a crisp and browned crust and a thin layer of the soft, pale dough inside against the meat.

All the seams and edges in a pâté en croûte must be carefully attended to. When you fit the dough into a rectangular mold, press it into the edges using a little piece of flour-dusted dough. Any two edges that come together must be well sealed. The top seam, formed when you fold the overhanging dough over the pâté to cover it, is the weakest edge, so pay close attention to it. When the mold goes into the oven, the farce itself can puff, or soufflé, and break the lid. With smaller pâté en croûte molds, the seam can run down the center, and the pâté can be unmolded and turned upside down in the mold so that the seam is on the bottom, resulting in a stronger crust.

MOISTURE BARRIER

What follows logically from a discussion of the crust is a strategy for keeping the pâté's moisture from making the dough soggy. It's important to protect the dough. Placing a layer of fat or thinly sliced protein between the raw dough and the meat is essential to a crisp crust and a perfectly cooked, fat-enriched meat filling. When meat cooks, juices can be squeezed out of the fat-protein meat emulsion. You want to keep these juices from compromising your crisp crust. You have several options:

CAUL FAT. One of the easiest and most effective moisture barriers is caul fat, the thin veil-like membrane that contains the viscera of a pig or cow. This is a single membrane of connective tissue, which gives a pâté an unbroken moisture barrier and is veined with fat to keep the pâté moist and succulent. Its only drawback is that home cooks may find it hard to come by; even chefs can have a difficult time finding it depending where they live and the regulations of slaughterhouses across the country. If you are able to find it, it's likely to be frozen. This is fine, as it freezes well, but it's best to let it thaw gradually in the refrigerator, then soak it in many changes of water to eliminate any blood and the odor of the viscera. Rinse it a few times a day until the liquid is clear instead of pink, then lay it out on a towel to dry before use.

THINLY SLICED BACK FAT. This is also a superb moisture barrier, because liquid can't penetrate the fat. But like caul fat, good, thick back fat can be difficult to find, and you will need to freeze it and slice it on an electric deli slicer to make paper-thin sheets.

THINLY SLICED HAM. This, of course, is widely available, and any grocery store deli counter can slice it paper-thin. You can use any ham—smoked or not, or even dried ham, such as prosciutto (though you might hold back a little on the salt since prosciutto is saltier than cooked ham). The drawback here is that ham doesn't adhere well and so can result in more air pockets than the two fats above.

BACON. We love to use thinly sliced bacon as a moisture barrier, especially in raised pies. Even if you don't have access to a deli slicer or a butcher who has one, you can put packaged bacon between plastic wrap and pound it as thin as possible. Bacon not only creates a barrier, it adds that fatty, smoky flavor everyone loves.

CRÊPES. For seafood pâtés or any vegetarian pies, Brian has had great success with crêpes. The protein in the egg, combined with the flour, creates an effective barrier. A fish pâté will have a higher moisture content, so a moisture barrier is especially important. Make individual crêpes as thin as possible in a large (12-inch/30-centimeter) pan.

Some en croûte molds are so small (1 inch/2.5 centimeters) that you don't need a moisture barrier. Because they're so small, you can cook them at a higher temperature, and moisture tends to be less of a problem.

OTHER CRITICAL ELEMENTS

FILLING THE MOLD. Fill it to the top and be sure to press out all air pockets as you do.

VENTING. As the pâté cooks, it will of course give off moisture. If the moisture isn't given an escape route, it will be absorbed by the crust, making it soggy. So, we cut vent holes in the top of the dough and insert a chimney, aluminum foil rolled into a cylinder. The holes also give us access to the interior so that after cooking, we can fill the space between the cooked pâté and the dough with aspic.

APPLYING EGG WASH. Whisk together 1 large egg, 1 large egg yolk, and 2 tablespoons milk and apply it to the dough before baking to give it color and shine.

COOKING. To ensure a good crust and a well-cooked interior, we begin with high heat, 450°F/230°C or so, and place the terrine in the middle of the oven to make sure the crust is good and browned. But that temperature would be too high for the pâté itself, so after about 25 minutes, we lower the temperature to 325°F/160°C so that the pâté cooks through without dropping all its fat. We keep track of the interior temperature with a thermometer. A cable thermometer, one that is inserted into the pâté at the beginning of cooking, is ideal so you don't have to keep opening the oven and making multiple punctures in the pâté each time you check its temperature. If you don't have a cable thermometer, try to pierce the pâté as few times as possible.

ADDING ASPIC. As the pâté cooks and cools, the meat will shrink, leaving a gap between it and the dough. We use some kind of aspic to fill the gap, typically a flavorful stock that we've clarified and added some gelatin to so that it is solid at room temperature. The aspic not only fills the gaps, giving the pâté en croûte structure, but adds flavor as well. The best time to add warm aspic to the pâté is after the pâté has had time to cool but is still warm, about 45 minutes after coming out of the oven.

UNMOLDING. The pâté should be thoroughly chilled before being unmolded. Sometimes aspic leaks through and sticks between the dough and the mold, making the pate difficult to unmold. It's a good idea to slightly warm the mold with a torch or, depending on your mold, with hot water, to melt the aspic before umolding.

SERVING. Cut the pâté en croûte into slices that are ½ to ¾ inch/12 to 20 millimeters thick and serve on a plate as you would a pâté en terrine: with mustard, cornichons, and salad or with any sauce, chutney, marmalade, or relish.

THE DOUGHS

The amount of fat affects the texture of a crust more than anything else. Fat shortens dough, preventing long strands of gluten, the protein in wheat flour, from forming. This is why bread is chewy and shortbread is crumbly. The traditional ratio for a standard pie crust, 3 parts flour to 2 parts fat to 1 part liquid, is often referred to as a 3-2-1 dough. Here we give the recipes for three doughs with varying fat contents:

Hot-Water Dough (15 percent fat)

Decker Dough (33 percent fat)

Pâte Brisée (40 percent fat)

The type of fat used also affects texture and flavor. Butter has water in it, which promotes the development of gluten, and thus affects texture that way. Lard does not contain water and so has a more powerful shortening effect. Butter has a sweet, rich flavor. Lard tends to be more savory, and if you have very good, fresh lard, it can even lend a pleasantly porky flavor to a dough.

A note should be made about the weight of flour relative to its volume—in other words, how much a cup of flour weighs. The answer is: It depends. It depends on how humid the air is, how long the flour has been sitting, and how the cup is filled. If the flour is poured into a cup then leveled, it will weigh less than if you scoop the flour in one go from flour that has sat for a while because the grains will be more compacted. In our experience a cup of flour has weighed as little as 4 ounces/110 grams and as much as 6 ounces/170 grams. If you are using cup measures only, and a recipe calls for ½ cup, it probably won't make a big difference.

But if you're using 4 cups of flour, as is sometimes called for in these recipes, it means you might be putting a pound of flour in your bowl *or* a pound and a half—a difference of 50 percent! This is why baking can be such a struggle for people—because they don't know how much flour they're adding. If you don't have a scale, we're not sure how you can be using this book, but as a rule of thumb, we estimate that a cup of flour weighs 5 ounces/140 grams. We urge you to always weigh your flour for the best results.

Dough should be worked just enough to bring all the elements together. Overworking dough can toughen it by developing the gluten. Once mixed, doughs should be chilled, with the exception of the Hot-Water Dough, which is rolled out while warm. When you are ready to use a chilled dough, it's best to remove it from the refrigerator 30 minutes before you roll it out. It should be stiff but still pliable.

Pâte Brisée

This is a very rich, buttery, all-purpose savory dough. It's great for raised pies, quiches, and tourtes. The weight of the flour is important so we urge you to use a scale here for the flour.

1 pound/450 grams (about 3¼ cups) all-purpose flour

1 tablespoon/15 grams kosher salt

1 pound/450 grams cold unsalted butter, cut into small dice

1 large egg

—

1. Combine the flour and salt in a large bowl. Add the butter and cut it into the flour and salt. Rub the mixture between your fingers until it resembles coarse meal.

2. Crack the egg into a liquid measuring cup. Add enough water so that the total volume equals 1 cup/240 milliliters, then whisk with a fork until they are uniformly blended.

3. Add the egg and water to the flour-butter mixture and mix by hand into a uniform paste.

4. Cover and chill for at least 1 hour. Remove from the refrigerator and let sit for 30 minutes before rolling.

YIELD: ABOUT 2½ POUNDS/1.1 KILOGRAMS DOUGH

Hot-Water Dough

This dough, made by melting fat in water, then adding the water and fat to the flour while still warm, results in a crisper crust. It's ideal for decorations on more fanciful pâtés en croûte and raised pies (about which more on page 150).

21 ounces/580 grams (about 4¼ cups) all-purpose flour

½ teaspoon/3 grams kosher salt

5 ounces/140 grams lard

1 cup/240 milliliters water

—

1. Sift the flour and salt into a bowl, then make a well in the center.

2. Combine the lard and water in a small saucepan and bring to a simmer over high heat. When the lard has melted, pour the warm water and lard into the well in the flour and mix to a paste.

3. Cover and let rest in a warm spot for 30 minutes before rolling.

YIELD: ABOUT 2 POUNDS/1 KILOGRAM DOUGH

Decker Dough

One of Brian's longtime friends and colleagues at Schoolcraft College is certified master pastry chef Joe Decker. Joe is that rare pastry chef who is equally adept in a savory kitchen as he is in a pastry kitchen. Most pastry chefs know how to make beautiful desserts; it's another skill altogether to make them both beautiful and delicious. Moreover, because at Schoolcraft Brian and his colleagues don't have the deadline pressures of running a restaurant, they can focus on perfecting their recipes. This is Joe's recipe for what we consider to be the perfect pastry crust for savory preparations.

We make this pâté dough in bulk because it freezes well. We shape it into a log and freeze it. Then we cut disks about 1 inch/2.5 centimeters thick as needed, rewrap the remaining dough, label and date it, and return it to the freezer (it will keep for about 3 months this way).

12 ounces/340 grams (about 2½ cups) all-purpose flour

½ teaspoon/3 grams kosher salt

4 ounces/110 grams unsalted butter, diced and chilled

4 ounces/110 grams lard, diced and chilled

½ cup/120 milliliters ice water

1 teaspoon distilled white vinegar

1. Combine the flour and salt in a large bowl. Add the butter and lard. Using both hands, pinch the fat into the flour and keep working it with your hands until the mixture resembles coarse meal; it should not become too warm or pasty.

2. Add the water and vinegar and mix until a dough forms.

3. Shape the dough into a log about 10 by 4 inches/25 by 10 centimeters. Wrap it in plastic wrap and refrigerate for at least 1 hour and up to 24 hours. Slice it into disks 1 inch/2.5 centimeters thick as needed. Let the disks sit at room temperature for 30 minutes before rolling.

YIELD: ABOUT 2 POUNDS/1 KILOGRAM DOUGH

NOTE: Although you can roll this dough out after an hour, it will still be very elastic. It's best to let this dough rest for at least 6 hours before rolling.

Rabbit Pâté en Croûte

We're providing only one pâté en croûte recipe because the method is the same no matter what forcemeat and garnish you use. Garnish should be abundant and be composed of different colors and shapes to give the slices of pâté a tantalizing mosaic. This is a preparation we really do eat with our eyes first, because it is relatively uncommon, and part of the purpose of going to the trouble of baking a pâté in a crust is for the beautiful presentation.

Brian loves using rabbit because it has a rich flavor and is so often overlooked. Many grocery stores now carry rabbit, and more farmers offer it at growers' markets. We urge you to try it, but you can certainly use duck or turkey instead.

The pâté en croûte is no different from a pâté en terrine, except that the mold is lined with dough. This recipe uses the Decker Dough, the one we recommend for all pâtés en croûte cooked in a mold. It's flexible and delicate but also strong, and it browns nicely.

As with all pâtés en croûte, this is cooked, then allowed to cool to the point that it's warm to the touch but not cold. At that point, warm aspic is poured into the crust to fill the space left as the pâté contracts. The aspic should be a richly flavored stock that you've clarified (see page 88).

Take care with each of the four components of the pâté en croûte—farce, garnish, crust, and aspic—and you will slice into one of the most rarefied preparations in charcuterie.

RECIPE CONTINUES ↱

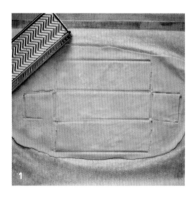

1: Mark out the dough with your pâté en croûte mold.
2: Place the dough in the mold. Line the mold with thinly sliced pork back fat.
3: Fill the mold with the forcemeat and fold the fat and then the crust over the top.
4: Create a vent hole and insert a chimney.
5: After the cooked pâté en croûte has cooled to room temperature, fill with aspic.

RABBIT PÂTÉ EN CROÛTE

FOR THE PÂTÉ:

2 tablespoons unsalted butter

1 tablespoon minced garlic

1 tablespoon minced shallot

½ cup/120 milliliters Madeira wine

12 ounces/340 grams lean rabbit meat from leg and thigh, trimmed of connective tissue and cut into 1-inch/2.5-centimeter dice

8 ounces/225 grams pork back fat, cut into 1-inch/2.5-centimeter dice

1½ tablespoons/22 grams kosher salt

1½ teaspoons freshly ground black pepper

1 tablespoon chopped fresh thyme leaves

1 tablespoon chopped fresh rosemary leaves

1 tablespoon chopped fresh flat-leaf parsley leaves

8 ounces/225 grams boneless, skinless chicken breast, cut into 1-inch/2.5-centimeter dice

¼ cup/60 milliliters brandy

1 large egg

½ cup/120 milliliters heavy cream

3 ounces/85 grams smoked beef tongue, cut into ¼-inch/6-millimeter dice

3 ounces/85 grams Duck Confit meat (page 163), coarsely chopped

3 ounces/85 grams shelled pistachios, coarsely chopped

FOR THE PÂTÉ EN CROUTE:

1½ pounds/680 grams Decker Dough (page 141), chilled

Vegetable oil or nonstick spray for greasing mold

16 paper-thin slices pork back fat, ham, or bacon

1 large egg

1 large egg yolk

2 tablespoons whole milk

FOR THE ASPIC:

¼ cup/60 milliliters cold water

1 tablespoon powdered gelatin

1½ cups/360 milliliters clarified duck or chicken stock (see page 88)

To make the pâté

1. In a small sauté pan, melt the butter over medium heat. Sweat the garlic and shallot until translucent but not browned, a minute or two. Deglaze with the Madeira, reduce by half, then remove the pan from the heat and let it cool.

2. Combine the diced rabbit and back fat in a bowl. Add the cooled Madeira mixture, salt, pepper, and herbs and toss to combine. Cover and marinate overnight.

3. In a separate bowl, toss the diced chicken breast with the brandy, cover, and marinate overnight.

4. The next day, remove the chicken breast from the brandy, reserving any residual liquid.

5. Remove the rabbit and pork fat from the marinade and reserve any residual liquid. Grind the rabbit and pork fat through a ⅛-inch/3-millimeter die into a metal bowl set in an ice bath. Transfer the mixture to a food processor, add the egg, and puree until smooth.

6. Do a quenelle test (see page 28) and adjust the seasoning if necessary, remembering that cooked food served cold requires extra attention. Return the pureed meat to the bowl, still in its ice bath. Add the cream, along with the reserved marinade from the chicken and rabbit. Using a rubber spatula, work the liquids into the meat until they are uniformly combined.

7. Fold in the garnish of tongue, duck confit, and pistachios, along with the marinated chicken breast. Cover and refrigerate until you are ready to fill the mold.

To make the pâté en croûte

1. Remove the dough from the refrigerator about 30 minutes before you are ready to work with it.

2. Grease the interior of a hinged metal pâté en croûte mold, about 10 by 3 by 3 inches/25 by 8 by 8 centimeters, with a removable bottom.

3. Pinch off a grape-size ball of dough and set aside. Roll the dough into a rectangle 20 by 14 inches/50 by 35 centimeters and ⅛ to ¼ inch/3 to 6 millimeters thick.

4. Carefully fold the dough in half lengthwise. Gently lay it in the mold, being careful not to tear the dough, and leave a 1-inch/2.5-centimeter overhang all the way around. Dust the ball of reserved dough with flour and use it to firmly press the dough rectangle into the corners of the mold.

5. To create a moisture barrier, line the dough with the thinly sliced back fat, overlapping each piece slightly. Fill the lined dough with the chilled forcemeat, packing it as tight as you can. Fold the dough over the forcemeat, trimming away excess dough with scissors as you go so that there is a slight overlap.

6. Whisk together the egg, egg yolk, and milk. Brush some of the egg wash over the surface of the dough that will overlap and form a seam. Fold it over to enclose the pâté (this will become the bottom of the pâté en croûte). Cover with plastic wrap and chill the pâté for at least 1 hour and up to 12 hours. Reserve the remaining egg wash in the refrigerator to brush on the pâté en croûte before you cook it. Wrap the reserved dough ball and reserve it in the refrigerator.

7. When you're ready to cook, preheat the oven to 400°F/200°C.

8. Remove the bottom of the pâté en croûte mold and reattach it on the seam side of the pâté en croûte, what had been the top.

9. Cut a 1-inch/2.5-centimeter hole in the center of the top so that steam can escape. To prevent the juices from overrunning the vent hole and darkening and burning the top of the crust, create an aluminum foil tube about 2 inches/5 centimeters long and wide enough to fit snugly into the hole in the center of the pâté en croûte. Insert it in the hole and use the reserved dough to create a ring around the vent hole for help supporting the chimney. Brush the new top with the reserved egg wash.

RECIPE CONTINUES ↪

10. Bake until the dough is beautifully brown, 20 to 30 minutes, then reduce the oven temperature to 300°F/150°C. Continue cooking to an internal temperature of 150°F/65°C; use the vent hole to check the temperature with an instant-read thermometer. Allow the pâté en croûte to rest for 45 minutes to an hour.

To make the aspic

1. Pour the cold water into a small saucepan and sprinkle the gelatin over it. Let it sit for 3 to 4 minutes to bloom (that is, absorb the water without forming clumps). Add the stock and warm over medium-low heat or in a microwave to dissolve the gelatin. Remove from the heat and allow the aspic to cool until it is warm but still liquid.

2. Using a funnel, slowly pour the warm aspic through the chimney to fill in the space left from meat shrinkage; you may not need it all. Refrigerate overnight before slicing and serving.

YIELD: 15 APPETIZER SERVINGS

Caramelized Onion Tart

The onion tart is a French bistro staple because it's made of simple ingredients, can be prepared in advance, and is equally delicious served warm, cold, or at room temperature. This dish is as much about the crust as the custard, so we use a rich pâte brisée, which is loaded with butter and blind baked (baked without the filling first). Very little egg and cream are used—really just enough to hold the onion together. The onion custard, topped with freshly grated Parmigiano-Reggiano, is almost like a garnish for the crust.

8 ounces/225 grams Pâte Brisée (page 140), chilled

¼ cup/60 grams unsalted butter

4 pounds/2 kilograms thinly sliced sweet onions

Kosher salt and freshly ground black pepper to taste

1 large egg

½ cup/120 milliliters heavy cream

4 ounces/120 grams grated Parmigiano-Reggiano

1. Preheat the oven to 350°F/175°C. Remove the dough from the refrigerator about 30 minutes before you are ready to work with it.

2. Roll the dough into a large (14-inch/ 35-centimeter) circle about ⅛ inch/ 3 millimeters thick. Lay the dough in an 11-inch/28-centimeter fluted tart pan with a removable bottom. Place a piece of parchment paper over the dough and fill it with pie weights or dried beans. Bake until golden brown, 20 to 30 minutes. Remove from the oven and allow to cool. Leave the oven on, or remember to preheat it again before baking the tart.

3. Melt the butter in a sauté pan over medium heat. Add the onions, season with salt and pepper, and cover with a tight-fitting lid. Cook until the onions are very soft, 10 to 15 minutes. Remove the lid, turn the heat to medium-high, and continue to cook, stirring, until the liquid cooks off and the onions turn golden brown. Remove from the heat and cool.

4. Spread the onions evenly over the crust. Whisk together the egg and cream, season with salt and pepper, and pour over the onions. Sprinkle the grated cheese evenly over the top. Bake until firm, about 25 minutes. Cool for at least 10 minutes before cutting into wedges to serve.

YIELD: 12 APPETIZER PORTIONS

Crab and Boursin Cheese Tart

Brian and I are from the Midwest, so fresh crab was never a part of our culinary heritage. But we've grown to love crab, and it's increasingly available freshly picked. Some canned brands are also excellent; be sure to look for lump or jumbo lump crab (not backfin). This tart combines the crabmeat with an ingredient that was definitely part of our 1970s culinary experience: Boursin, a rich, garlicky spreadable cheese created from a mild cow's milk cheese in Normandy. The tart combines the two simpatico ingredients, unified by a rich crust.

8 ounces/225 grams Pâte Brisée (page 140), chilled

1 pound/450 grams Maryland jumbo crabmeat

½ cup/110 grams diced red bell pepper

3 scallions (white and pale green parts only), sliced thin

4 ounces/120 grams Boursin cheese

1 large egg

½ cup/120 milliliters heavy cream

Kosher salt and freshly ground black pepper to taste

Grated nutmeg to taste

1. Preheat the oven to 350°F/175°C. Remove the dough from the refrigerator about 30 minutes before you are ready to work with it.

2. Roll the dough into a large (14-inch/35-centimeter) circle about ⅛ inch/3 millimeters thick. Lay the dough in an 11-inch/28-centimeter fluted tart pan with a removable bottom. Place a piece of parchment paper over the dough and fill it with pie weights or dried beans. Bake until golden brown, 20 to 30 minutes. Remove from the oven and allow to cool. Leave the oven on, or remember to preheat it again before baking the tart.

3. Put the crab in a bowl and pick through it to ensure there are no bits of shells. Add the red pepper, scallions, and Boursin. Mix gently until the ingredients are uniformly combined.

4. Crack the egg into the mix and stir in the cream. Season with salt, pepper, and nutmeg to taste.

5. Carefully pour the mixture over the crust and spread evenly. Bake until the custard is set, 20 to 30 minutes. Cool for at least 20 minutes before cutting into wedges to serve.

YIELD: 8 APPETIZER PORTIONS

Savory Sweet Potato Tart

This tart works perfectly for Thanksgiving but also makes a terrific everyday side dish for a roasted chicken or beef roast. Brian loves what it represents about cooking: how, with a little bit of craft, a simple vegetable can be transformed into an elegant dish.

2 pounds/1 kilogram sweet potatoes

8 ounces/225 grams Pâte Brisée (page 140), chilled

½ cup/115 grams unsalted butter, at room temperature

Kosher salt and freshly ground black pepper to taste

Grated nutmeg to taste

2 large eggs

½ cup/120 milliliters heavy cream

1. Preheat the oven to 425°F/218°C.

2. Roast the sweet potatoes until tender, about 1 hour. Let them cool until you can peel them comfortably. Reduce the oven temperature to 350°F/175°C. Remove the dough from the refrigerator about 30 minutes before you are ready to work with it.

3. Roll the dough into a large (14-inch/ 35-centimeter) circle about ⅛ inch/ 3 millimeters thick. Lay the dough in an 11-inch/28-centimeter fluted tart pan with a removable bottom. Place a piece of parchment paper over the dough and fill it with pie weights or dried beans. Bake until golden brown, 20 to 30 minutes. Remove from the oven and allow to cool. Leave the oven on, or remember to preheat it again before baking the tart.

4. Put the peeled sweet potatoes in a food processor, along with the butter, salt, pepper, and nutmeg, and puree until smooth. Taste for seasoning and adjust it, keeping in mind that eggs and cream will still be added. With the machine running, add the eggs, one at a time. Transfer the puree to a mixing bowl.

5. Lightly whip the cream to just barely soft peaks—it should almost be runny. Fold it gently into the sweet potato mixture.

6. Pour the mixture over the crust and spread evenly. Bake until set, about 20 minutes. Cut into wedges and serve warm.

YIELD: 8 TO 12 APPETIZER PORTIONS

Raised Tongue Pie

A raised pie is a British term that typically refers to a tall meat pie. We use it here to designate a forcemeat wrapped in dough and cooked, then sliced to serve. It's a very easy way to make en croûte dishes. This is a crispy-crusted pie thanks to the hot-water dough. For this pie, Brian covers the top seam with an extra layer of dough because this dough is extra crispy. (For the Raised Pheasant Pie on page 153, you simply flip the seam to the bottom, but this dough and this technique can also be used for that pie, and vice versa.) This pie is a great vehicle for an underused but delicious preparation, smoked tongue; here, it's suspended in a straight pork forcemeat. The smoky flavor from the bacon and tongue makes for a great autumn Sunday brunch dish. Remember that even though tongue may be smoked, this doesn't mean it's cooked all the way through. Ask your butcher if it needs further cooking.

1 pound/450 grams Hot-Water Dough (page 140), at room temperature

12 ounces/340 grams thinly sliced bacon

1 pound/450 grams Classic Pork Pâté (page 39)

14 ounces/400 grams smoked, cooked beef or veal tongue, cut lengthwise into ¼-inch/6-millimeter pieces

1 large egg

1 large egg yolk

2 tablespoons whole milk

—

1. Preheat the oven to 375°F/190°C.

2. On a sheet of parchment paper, roll the dough into a rectangle about 15 by 18 inches/38 by 45 centimeters. Turn the dough so that the longer sides are parallel to the edge of the work surface.

3. Starting 2 inches/5 centimeters from the lower left corner, shingle all the bacon slices vertically from left to right to form an unbroken moister barrier, stopping 2 inches/5 centimeters from the lower right corner. There will be an unused rectangle of dough across the top, about 4 by 18 inches/10 by 45 centimeters; cut this off and reserve to cover the seam on top.

4. Spread a layer of forcemeat, about 4 inches/10 centimeters long and ½ inch/1 centimeter wide, vertically down the center of the bacon slices. Arrange a layer of tongue strips over the forcemeat. Spread another layer of forcemeat on top of the tongue, and then make another layer of tongue. Repeat the process until you have 6 layers of forcemeat and 5 layers of tongue.

5. Holding the left side of the parchment paper, roll the dough and bacon up and over the vertical log of forcemeat and tongue. Do the same on the other side, so that they overlap. Pinch the ends of the dough and trim excess dough.

6. Whisk together the egg, egg yolk and milk. Brush the top of the dough with some of the egg wash and place the reserved dough rectangle on top to cover the seam. Brush that piece of dough with the remaining egg wash. Transfer the parchment and pie to a rimmed baking sheet and bake until the internal temperature reaches 145°F/63°C and the crust is browned and crisp, 30 to 45 minutes.

7. Slice and serve immediately, or cool, cover, and refrigerate until ready to serve.

YIELD: 8 APPETIZER PORTIONS

RAISED PHEASANT PIE

Raised Pheasant Pie

Pheasant is a meat that many hunters aren't sure what to do with, so Brian wanted to offer this raised pie (a British term for a tall meat pie). You can also use turkey, or of course chicken. If you prefer not to use sweetbreads as a garnish, feel free to use whatever you like— mushrooms, bacon lardons, or any other appropriate garnish (see page 32). In this recipe we flip the pie over so the dough seam will be on the bottom, but you can use the technique described for the Raised Tongue Pie (page 150) if you prefer.

1 (2- to 3-pound/1- to 1.5-kilogram) whole pheasant (or 8 ounces/ 225 grams turkey leg and thigh meat plus 12 ounces/340 grams turkey breast meat)

6 to 8 ounces/ 170 to 225 grams pork back fat as needed

1 pound/450 grams Pâté Brisée (page 140), at room temperature

12 ounces/340 grams thinly sliced bacon

1 tablespoon unsalted butter

2 tablespoons minced garlic

2 tablespoons minced shallot

½ cup/120 milliliters dry sherry

2 large eggs

Kosher salt and freshly ground black pepper to taste

½ cup/120 milliliters heavy cream

3 ounce/85 grams cooked sweetbreads (see page 65), broken into pieces

2 ounces/60 grams smoked tongue, cut into ½-inch/ 1-centimeter dice

2 ounces/60 grams blanched peeled pistachios

1 large egg yolk

2 tablespoons whole milk

1. Bone the pheasant legs and thighs, discarding all skin, fat, bone, and sinew. Remove the breast, trim and reserve the tenderloins, and discard all skin, fat, bone, and sinew. Dice the breast meat.

2. Weigh the legs, thighs, and tenderloins; you should have 8 to 10 ounces/225 to 280 grams (reserve any excess for another use). Dice the meat. To determine the amount of pork back fat needed, multiply the weight of the dark meat by 0.8 and weigh out that amount in back fat. Dice the back fat. Refrigerate all the meat.

3. Preheat the oven to 375°F/190°C.

4. On a sheet of parchment paper, roll the dough into a rectangle about 15 by 18 inches/38 by 45 centimeters. Turn the dough so that the longer sides are parallel to the edge of the work surface.

5. Starting 2 inches/5 centimeters from the lower left corner, shingle all the bacon slices vertically from left to right to form an unbroken moisture barrier, stopping 2 inches/5 centimeters from the lower right corner. The strips of dough at the bottom and top not covered by bacon will be pinched together to seal the pie.

6. Melt the butter in a sauté pan over medium heat. Sauté the garlic and shallot until translucent, then add the sherry and reduce it to a syrup. Cool the reduction to room temperature.

RECIPE CONTINUES ➤

7. Grind the pheasant dark meat and back fat through a ⅛-inch/3-millimeter die into a metal bowl set in an ice bath. Transfer to a food processor and add the cooled reduction, 1 egg, and salt and pepper. Puree until smooth. Transfer the puree to a bowl and fold in the cream with a rubber spatula. Add the diced breast meat, sweetbreads, tongue, and pistachios and stir until uniformly combined.

8. Spread the forcemeat vertically down the center of the bacon slices in a log about the diameter of a lemon.

9. Holding the parchment paper, roll the dough and bacon up around the log, from both top and bottom, bringing the edges of the dough together and pinching them to seal it. Trim any excess dough and flip the pie over so that the seam is on the bottom.

10. Whisk together the remaining 1 egg, egg yolk, and milk. Brush the entire pie with the egg wash. Using kitchen shears, snip several ½-inch/1-centimeter vents along the top of the dough to allow steam to escape.

11. Place the parchment and roll on a rimmed baking sheet and bake until the internal temperature reaches 145°F/63°C and the crust is browned and crisp, 30 to 45 minutes.

12. Slice and serve immediately, or cool, cover, and refrigerate until ready to serve.

YIELD: 8 APPETIZER PORTIONS

Savory Duck Pies

These individual-size pies are a really cool make-ahead dish for when friends come over, as they can be prepared the day before; just pop them in the oven to reheat and toss a salad. It's a great way to get people thinking about good food in America, as this is so special and yet so easy to prepare ahead of time. Brian recently had these on the menu at Schoolcraft College's American Harvest restaurant. He uses small tart pans, but if you don't have these, use one of the "raised pie" techniques for enclosing the duck pâté (pages 150 and 153).

1½ pounds/680 grams Pâte Brisée (page 140), chilled

1 (5-pound/2.25-kilogram) whole duck

10 ounces/280 grams pork back fat, cut into 1-inch/2.5-centimeter dice

5 ounces/140 grams pork butt, cut into 1-inch/2.5-centimeter dice

2 large eggs

All-Purpose Spice Mix for Meat Pâtés (page 33) to taste

Kosher salt and freshly ground black pepper to taste

8 ounces/225 grams smoked ham, cut into ½-inch/1-centimeter dice

Caul fat as needed (see page 137)

1 large egg yolk

2 tablespoons whole milk

1. Remove the dough from the refrigerator about 30 minutes before you are ready to work with it.

2. Remove the legs from the duck. Remove the skin and reserve, then bone the legs (reserve the bones for stock if you wish). Remove any sinew from the meat. Weigh the leg meat; you should have around 10 ounces/280 grams (in the event that you don't have that weight, supplement it with additional pork butt). Cut the meat into 1-inch/2.5-centimeter dice.

3. Remove the skin from the rest of the duck and reserve. Remove the breast halves from the carcass and cut into ½-inch/1-centimeter dice. (Reserve the carcass, wings, and neck for stock if you wish.)

4. Cut all the skin into ½-inch/ 1-centimeter pieces.

5. Grind the leg meat, back fat, and pork butt through a ⅛-inch/3-millimeter die into a metal bowl set in an ice bath. Transfer to a food processor and add 1 egg; season with the spice mix and salt and pepper to taste. Puree until smooth. Transfer the mixture to a bowl, then fold in the ham and duck breast.

6. Preheat the oven to 400°F/205°C.

RECIPE CONTINUES ➔

Crust

7. Weigh out six 3-ounce/85-gram dough balls. Roll them into 7-inch/17-centimeter rounds. Line six 5-inch/12-centimeter fluted tart shells with removable bottoms with the dough, leaving a ¼-inch/6-millimeter overhang all around.

8. Line the dough with a veil of caul fat to serve as a moisture barrier. Fill the shells with the duck mixture, then smooth out the top. Divide the remaining dough into six equal portions. Roll them into 5-inch/12-centimeter rounds and top the tarts with them, using water to seal the top and bottom crusts. Trim the dough to go just past the edge of the tart pan. With your thumb and forefinger on one hand and forefinger on the other, crimp the edges all around.

9. Whisk together the remaining 1 egg, egg yolk, and milk. Snip steam vents in the tops of the pies with scissors, then brush with the egg wash. Bake until they reach an internal temperature of 140°F/60°C and the dough is nice and brown, 15 to 20 minutes. Let rest for 15 minutes before serving.

YIELD: 6 INDIVIDUAL PIES

Wild Mushroom Tourte

This is a free-form pie or log, not unlike the "raised pies," and a great example of how good dough makes a dish. *Tourte* is a French term used by Brian's mentor, Milos Cihelka, that denotes an enclosed tart. It's very easy to prepare for an elegant appetizer. Make it ahead of time and refrigerate, then bake, slice, and serve. Since this is meant to be an appetizer, the diameter of the log should be no larger than a soup can—a little smaller, in fact—and it can be as long as the sheet pan it cooks on. Choose fresh, in-season wild mushrooms, such as chanterelles, hedgehogs, morels, oysters, or shiitakes. You can certainly use cultivated button or cremini (baby portobello) mushrooms— but then don't call this tart wild!

12 ounces/340 grams Pâte Brisée (page 140), chilled

¼ cup/60 grams unsalted butter

1 pound/450 grams mixed wild mushrooms, cleaned and roughly chopped

2 tablespoons minced shallot

½ cup/120 milliliters dry sherry

½ cup/60 grams all-purpose flour

½ cup/120 milliliters heavy cream

3 tablespoons chopped fresh flat-leaf parsley

1 large egg

1 large egg yolk

2 tablespoons whole milk

1. Preheat the oven to 350°F/175°C. Remove the dough from the refrigerator about 30 minutes before you are ready to work with it.

2. Melt the butter in a sauté pan over medium-high heat. Add the mushrooms and shallot and cook until their moisture is released. Add the sherry and turn the heat to high. Cook until all the moisture has evaporated. Dust with the flour, cook for another minute or so, then add the cream. Turn the heat to medium-low and cook gently until the cream has reduced and the mixture thickens. Remove from the heat and allow to cool to room temperature, then add the parsley. It should be thick enough to shape.

3. On a sheet of parchment paper, roll the dough into a rectangle 14 by 6 inches/ 35 by 15 centimeters. Turn the dough so that the longer sides are parallel to the edge of the work surface. Spread the mushroom mixture all the way across the center of the dough, leaving a border all around the edges. Carefully lift the dough from the bottom edge and roll it over the mushroom mixture to create a log. Pinch the dough edges together to seal, then transfer the parchment and log to a rimmed baking sheet, seam side down.

4. Whisk together the egg, egg yolk, and milk. Brush the log with the egg wash. Using kitchen shears, snip several ½-inch/1-centimeter vents along the top of the dough to allow steam to escape. Bake until the dough is nice and brown and the filling is hot, 25 to 30 minutes. Slice and serve hot.

YIELD: 12 APPETIZER PORTIONS

PART 5

The Mighty Confit

Gascony, the southwestern corner of France (where d'Artagnan of *The Three Musketeers* and Armagnac were born), is the spiritual home of the equally robust confit, that tantalizing and bountiful technique of taking a rich, fatty piece of meat, poaching it in more fat, then storing it submerged in that fat for a week or a month or many months or even years.

In Gascony, confit was more than a great way to prepare goose and duck—it meant survival. Before refrigeration, families would put up enough confit to last through a winter and store it on some cool, out-of-the-way shelf. Historically, though, they wouldn't eat *this* confit during the upcoming winter. It would sit on the shelf untouched throughout the winter and then through the summer and through the fall, while they put up more duck and goose confit. They would eat the confit from the previous year only once they'd put up a new batch, to ensure that they had enough food for this year and the next. Some might eat the confit from two years before.

Duck confit is one of my favorite things to cook and to eat, and when I learned that humans had devised the confit not for their own pleasure, but rather for their survival—so that they would have food all winter long—it took a front-row seat in my heart. That the ingenuity required to survive the winter resulted in a culinary marvel we still love today, even though we don't need to preserve it, makes me revere it as I do few foods.

Of course, the very qualities of preservation that make confit a great survival strategy are useful in our post-refrigeration lives for the same reason. Confit stays good for months and months—indeed, it gets better with time. This means that if you confited 12 duck legs in November and forgot about them in the back of the fridge, you've got several weeknight dinners ready to crisp under a broiler and serve in January, February, and March. Home late after a busy day at work? Duck confit, a salad, and some crusty bread is a great meal that's ready in a flash.

Or if you have unexpected company, you've got a four-star meal at the ready. Serve it as its own course, or turn a few of those legs into rillettes (page 187). It takes five minutes and you've got fabulous food to set out with some toast, cornichons, mustard, and red wine for everyone to enjoy.

While pork wasn't traditionally confited for preservation, it makes a fabulous confit. The pig was preserved in different ways than being cooked and stored in fat, most commonly by salting and drying it, but the shoulder and the belly lend themselves beautifully to the confit technique. Especially the belly. And especially when you season it with great spices and herbs.

Chicken is rarely preserved, but why not confit chicken wings and legs for your own pleasure? (You could confit a chicken breast if you wanted to, but it's going to be a little dry and mealy in texture—so there's really no point in doing so.) A confited chicken thigh is deeply satisfying.

And, well, why not turkey, that underappreciated meat? Turkey confit is fabulous! And it's a great way to have extra turkey to offer at Thanksgiving. Make it a week (or months) in advance and don't worry about having enough turkey on the big day. And once you make if for Thanksgiving, you'll want to make it all year.

Why is confit so good, especially for meats? In a way it's like a braise—meat cooked low and slow in a fluid environment. But unlike a braise, which uses water, stock, or wine, the cooking environment accomplishes the job of cooking and tenderizing the meat without drawing out the flavor. Meat and bones cooked in water eventually lose all their flavor to that water. But not so with confit. The water in the skin cooks off; the gelatin from the skin, cartilage, and bones is released and sinks to the bottom. This intensely flavored, salty protein can be drizzled over the crisped duck or added to a vinaigrette. And the duck itself—or pork, or chicken, or turkey—maintains all its savory essence.

Duck Confit

(MASTER CONFIT RECIPE)

Meat confits can be cooked in the oven or on the stovetop. If you have access to sous vide equipment, this too is a very efficient way to achieve the effects of confit. (Vegetable confits can vary slightly, depending on the item, but all are by definition cooked in fat.) All our meat confits follow the same basic method.

STEP 1: Salt and season the duck legs. Traditionally, confit was heavily salted, sometimes packed in salt, in order to begin the preservation process. Salt would pull water from the duck and disable spoilage bacteria. Today we give the meat an aggressive salting but mainly as a seasoning device. We also add spices and aromatics. This can be as simple as pepper, or you can add garlic and thyme for more flavor. But you can also go in any seasoning direction you like. Say you want an Asian-style confit—you could drizzle the meat with soy sauce and add ginger, garlic, scallions, and five-spice powder. Or you could take it in a more western European direction with allspice and cinnamon. Fat carries all flavors beautifully. Allow the salt and seasonings to work their magic for at least 8 hours, but preferably for a full day or two.

STEP 2: Put the legs in an appropriate cooking vessel and cover them with fat. Choose an oven-safe pot that's taller than it is wide, which will minimize the amount of fat you'll need. The legs can be layered as long as they're all submerged in the fat. They will plump in the early stages

of cooking, so you do need to be generous with the fat at the outset.

Traditionally duck fat would be rendered and used to cook the duck, and this remains by far the best fat to use. It's possible to get enough fat from a single duck to confit that duck, even though ducks here tend to be leaner than their Gascon relatives. But most of us buy our duck legs individually, either online, at a butcher's, or from local farmers if we are so lucky. Duck fat can also be bought, often from the same purveyors.

But other fats work as well. Ideally, you want a fat that is solid at room temperature because it is better at preventing air from reaching the meat. This means pork fat, or lard, would be the next-best choice for confit. But any fat will work for those who don't have easy access to duck or pork fat. Olive oil is perhaps the best fat for home cooks in terms of both convenience and flavor. It works great and tastes delicious. Vegetable oil or shortening will work, but these fats have no flavor and thus can result in confit that feels a bit insipid, so be sure to season the meat aggressively.

STEP 3: Confit the duck. Preheat the oven to 200°F/93°C (or 180°F/82°C, if your oven goes that low). If using solid fat, melt the fat over medium heat, then add the duck legs; if using olive oil, put the duck legs in the pot and pour the oil over them. Bring the fat up to 180°F/82°C, then transfer the pot, uncovered, to the oven. Cook until done, 4 to 6 hours. There are two reliable visible indicators that the confit is done: First, duck legs will float slightly when raw, but when all the water and air have cooked out of the skin, they will sink to the bottom of the pan. Second, during the cooking, the fat will be cloudy; when the legs are done, the fat will be clear. So when you see the legs sharply, through the oil, resting on the bottom of the pan, they are done.

Brian likes to cook his confit entirely on the stovetop, partly because he likes to keep an eye on it but more importantly because in a restaurant kitchen, oven space is at a premium and you don't want to tie it up with something that can be prepared on top of the stove. I prefer to start mine on the stovetop and then transfer it to the oven because I don't want to have to keep an eye on it. Also, I find the oven method more consistent and, frankly, easier. If you prefer to use the stovetop, bring the oil up to 180°F/82°C and then maintain that temperature until the confit is done. It will take the same amount of time, 4 to 6 hours.

(As noted, if you have the capacity to sous vide, you can bag your duck legs with the salt and aromatics and cook them at 180°F/82°C for 12 hours, then chill them in an ice bath in the bag.)

STEP 4: CHILL THE CONFIT. This can be as simple as letting the pan cool to room temperature and then refrigerating it. What's even better, though, is to transfer the hot duck to a heat-proof container and then pour the hot fat over it until it is completely submerged, reserving the flavorful gelatin at the bottom of the cooking pan, and then refrigerating (the gelatin will keep, refrigerated, for about a week). But the important part is to allow it to chill thoroughly while submerged in the fat.

STEP 5: Wait to eat it. This is the hard part, but the longer the duck stays in this fat, the better it will taste. Chefs like to say that it ripens in the fat. But from a practical standpoint, you need only wait until the fat has completely congealed.

STEP 6: Cook the confit. Remove the duck legs from the fat and let them come to room temperature if you have time. Pour a good layer of the cooking fat into a sauté pan to prevent the skin from sticking and tearing. Wipe the excess fat off the legs and place them, skin side up, in the pan. Cook the legs in a 350°F/175°C oven until they're heated through, about 15 minutes.

Then put them under the broiler for a few minutes to crisp the skin.

Many of the pâtés in this book suggest adding duck confit to the forcemeat—it does make an excellent interior garnish. Or you can turn the confit into rillettes (see page 187). The confit, of course, can also be added to a bean stew, as is traditional in Gascony, famed for its cassoulet. I'm guessing that this was initially a necessary strategy as the duck would have been heavily salted for preservation, too salty to eat on its own as we do now, and cooking it in beans would leach out the salt and season the stew. Now we would cook them in the stew for their deliciousness.

STEP 7: Store the confit. Any leftover confit can be stored as is in an airtight container or zip-top bag. It will keep in the refrigerator for a week or so. If you want to ensure that it keeps for many months, be sure that it is completely submerged in the fat so that no air touches it. It will keep in the refrigerator for six months or more this way. If mold appears, or if the confit is discolored or has an off smell, it has been improperly stored and probably shouldn't be eaten.

＞＞•＞•◆•＜•＜＜

The following recipe is the basic duck confit method, but it shows how all the meat confits in this book are prepared. Use as many or as few duck legs as you wish. We prefer many, a dozen or so, because duck confit is so delicious and so versatile to have on hand, especially throughout the cold winter.

In terms of the amounts of other ingredients, use your common sense. Salt each duck leg—use about ½ teaspoon per leg. Grind pepper over them as desired, or use whole black peppercorns well crushed beneath a sauté pan. Use a clove of garlic per leg if you like garlic. Use a sprig or two of thyme per leg if you like thyme. You'll need about 1 quart/1 liter of fat to cover a dozen legs. And that's all there is to it.

> **Whole duck legs**
>
> **Kosher salt and freshly ground black pepper**
>
> **Garlic cloves, lightly smashed**
>
> **Fresh thyme sprigs**
>
> **Rendered duck fat, lard, or extra virgin olive oil**

RECIPE CONTINUES ↪

1. Season the duck legs with salt and pepper, then put them in a large container or one or more zip-top plastic bags. Scatter the garlic and thyme over them. Cover the container or seal the bags and refrigerate for at least 8 hours or up to 3 days.

2. Preheat the oven to 200°F/93°C (or 180°F/82°C, if your oven goes that low).

3. Choose a pot or Dutch oven in which the duck legs will fit snugly; ideally it will be taller than it is wide. Melt the fat over medium heat.

4. Rinse the duck with cold water and pat dry with paper towels.

5. When the fat is melted, add the duck, making sure it is submerged. If it's not, add more fat. Bring the fat up to 180°F/82°C, then transfer the pot, uncovered, to the oven. (Alternatively, you can lower the heat to maintain that temperature and continue cooking on the stovetop.) Cook until the legs sink to the bottom of the pot and the fat is clear, 4 to 6 hours.

6. Cool the duck in the fat, then store as described on page 165, step 7.

YIELD (PER DUCK LEG): 1 SERVING AS AN ENTRÉE OR 2 TO 3 SERVINGS AS RILLETTES

Goose Confit

Confit d'oie is a specialty of southwestern France, but it's found all over that country, especially where fowl are raised for foie gras. This recipe is simple but luscious. Try to find a fresh (rather than frozen) bird, which is more likely to be available around the holidays.

> 1 (10- to 12-pound/4.5- to 5.5-kilogram) whole goose
>
> ⅔ cup/150 grams kosher salt
>
> 20 whole black peppercorns
>
> 12 garlic cloves, lightly smashed
>
> 1 large bunch fresh thyme
>
> 4 bay leaves
>
> ½ cup/120 milliliters water
>
> Additional rendered goose fat, rendered duck fat, and/or lard as needed

Day One

1. Trim the bird of all loose skin and fat, especially the neck skin and fat near the tail, and reserve for rendering. Remove the leg from each side of the bird, and separate the drumsticks from the thighs. Using a heavy knife or cleaver, cut off the knobby end of each drumstick (this will allow the meat to ride up the bone into a more compact muscle, leaving one end of the bone clean for a more appealing presentation).

2. Cut off the outer two-thirds of each wing (the tip and flat) and reserve for stock if desired. Remove each drumette from the breast by slicing into the fat end of the breast in a broad circle above the wing joint to capture a large chunk of breast meat along with the drumette itself for a meaty portion, then separate the ball joint to detach the wing from the carcass.

3. Stand the goose on end, neck side down, and slice through the rib cage just below the meat to separate the backbone from the breastbones. Using a heavy knife or cleaver, cut the breast in half along the keel bone. Cut each breast half in half crosswise, so that you have four roughly equal pieces of breast on the bone. Trim all pieces of excess skin, protruding breastbones, and fat and add the trimmings to the other reserved skin and fat. (Reserve the bones for stock, if you wish.)

4. Put the 10 pieces of goose in a baking pan and add the salt, peppercorns, garlic, thyme, and bay leaves. Rub the ingredients all over the goose, cover, and refrigerator for at least 8 hours or up to 3 days.

5. Meanwhile, put the reserved skin and fat in a large saucepan, add the water, and cook over low heat until the fat is rendered and clear. Strain the fat and save the cracklings for another use (garnish for a salad, for instance). You should have about 3 quarts/3 liters of strained fat. Cover and refrigerate.

RECIPE CONTINUES ↻

Day Two

1. Preheat the oven to 200°F/93°C (or 180°F/82°C, if your oven goes that low).

2. Choose a pot or Dutch oven in which the goose will fit snugly; ideally it will be taller than it is wide. Melt the fat over medium heat.

3. Remove the goose from the refrigerator, rinse the pieces with cold water, and pat dry with a paper towel.

4. When the fat is melted, add the goose to the pot. The pieces must be completely submerged in the fat. If they're not, add more fat. Bring the fat up to 180°F/82°C, then transfer the pot, uncovered, to the oven. (Alternatively, you can lower the heat to maintain that temperature and continue cooking on the stovetop.) Cook until the goose and its juices have sunk to the bottom of the pot and the fat is clear, 4 to 6 hours.

5. Cool the goose in the fat, then store as described on page 165, step 7.

YIELD: 10 ENTRÉE PORTIONS

Pork Belly Confit

This is a preparation Brian uses often in his restaurants, when a slice of belly is one component on a composed plate. He weights it after cooking so that he can cut uniform rectangular portions that cook evenly. Of course, this same recipe and technique will work for a belly precut into portions before cooking and stored in the fat as with a traditional confit. We don't recommend you confit skin-on belly because when you reheat it, the skin will spatter and pop from moisture within the skin (see how we handle pork skin for Cracklings, page 221, and Chicharrón, page 220). This preparation works well served with roasted pork loin, spicy greens, or braised lentils.

¼ cup/60 grams kosher salt

1 tablespoon whole black peppercorns

1 tablespoon coriander seeds

2 bay leaves

1 bunch fresh thyme

2 garlic cloves, lightly smashed

3 pounds/1.5 kilograms pork belly, edges trimmed so that it is squared off

2 quarts/2 liters lard or extra virgin olive oil, or more as needed

1. Combine the salt, peppercorns, coriander, bay leaves, thyme sprigs, and garlic in a bowl or zip-top plastic bag and stir to mix. Add the pork belly and rub the mixture evenly all over it. Cover the bowl or seal the bag and refrigerate for 3 days.

2. Choose a pot or Dutch oven in which the pork belly will fit snugly; ideally it will be taller than it is wide. Melt the lard over medium heat.

3. Rinse the belly with cold water and pat dry with paper towels.

4. When the fat is melted, add the belly, making sure it is submerged in the fat. If it's not, add more fat. Bring the fat to 180°F/82°C and cook the belly until fork-tender, about 3 hours, adjusting the heat as necessary to maintain the temperature of the fat at all times.

5. Transfer the belly to a baking pan and cover with plastic wrap (reserve the lard for cooking or confiting). Place another pan on top and weight it with several cans so that it maintains a uniform thickness. Refrigerate until chilled, at least a couple of hours.

6. To serve, cut the belly into 3-inch/8-centimeter squares and pan-fry, deep-fry, or roast in the oven until hot in the center.

YIELD: 8 APPETIZER PORTIONS

Carolina BBQ Pork Confit

This confit, which has seasonings associated with barbecue, is great for roasting as a steak after it's cooked and chilled. Ask your butcher to cut 1-inch/2.5-centimeter slabs from a pork butt, or cut your own. The fun is in having a steak-like cut, an atypical way to use pork shoulder. Serve it with roasted corn on the cob, vegetable slaw, and a vinegar-based barbecue sauce.

FOR THE DRY RUB:

6 tablespoons/90 grams kosher salt

¼ cup smoked hot paprika (preferably pimentón de la Vera)

¼ cup ground coriander

3 tablespoons chili powder

2 tablespoons light brown sugar

2 tablespoons dried oregano

2 tablespoons freshly ground black pepper

2 tablespoons ground white pepper

2 teaspoons cayenne pepper

FOR THE CONFIT:

2 tablespoons/30 grams kosher salt

3 (1½-pound/680-gram) pork "steaks," cut from well-marbled shoulder, about 9 by 4 inches/22 by 10 centimeters and 1 inch/2.5 centimeters thick

1 quart/1 liter vegetable oil

1. Combine all the dry rub ingredients and mix until uniformly combined. Measure out ¼ cup for this recipe and transfer to a small bowl. (Store the remainder in an airtight container at room temperature for up to 3 weeks or in the freezer for up to 3 months. Use it on future batches of confit or on roasted or grilled pork.)

2. To prep the confit, mix the additional kosher salt with the reserved dry rub and rub it evenly all over the pork steaks. Put the steaks in a zip-top plastic bag, seal, and refrigerate for 2 days.

3. Preheat the oven to 200°F/93°C (or 180°F/82°C, if your oven goes that low).

4. Choose a pot or Dutch oven in which the steaks will fit snugly; ideally it will be taller than it is wide. Rinse the steaks with cold water and pat dry with paper towels. Put the steaks in the pot and cover them with the oil.

5. Bring the oil up to 180°F/82°C over medium heat, then transfer the pot, uncovered, to the oven. (Alternatively, you can lower the heat to maintain that temperature and continue cooking on the stovetop.) Cook until tender, about 4 hours.

6. Allow the pork to cool in the fat, then refrigerate it until you're ready to reheat to serve.

YIELD: 6 ENTRÉE PORTIONS OR 12 APPETIZER PORTIONS

Pork Shoulder Confit

Confit can change your life. It did mine. It did Brian's. Confit, especially pork confit, is a very versatile component. It can be used as an interior garnish for terrines, turned into rillettes (see page 187), or eaten on its own as a snack or main course for dinner. At Brian's Forest Grill, he used to marinate the pork for 3 days, slowly cook it in fat until tender, then press it while cooling between two sheet pans. This gave him a fully cooked pavé of pork that he could deep-fry at the last minute and serve with roasted bone marrow, an arugula salad, and chorizo spuma. It was fantastic. This recipe, like the Carolina BBQ Pork Confit (page 171), uses pork shoulder "steaks"; cut your own or ask a butcher to do it for you.

2 tablespoons/30 grams kosher salt

20 whole black peppercorns

4 garlic cloves, lightly smashed

3 tablespoons chopped shallot

3 bay leaves

1 bunch fresh thyme

3 (1½-pound/680-gram) pork "steaks," cut from well-marbled shoulder, about 9 by 4 inches/22 by 10 centimeters and 1 inch/2.5 centimeters thick

1 quart/1 liter rendered duck fat and/or lard

1. Combine the salt, peppercorns, garlic, shallot, bay leaves, and thyme sprigs and mix well. Rub the seasoning mixture all over the pork steaks. Put the steaks in a zip-top plastic bag, seal, and refrigerate for 2 to 3 days.

2. Preheat the oven to 200°F/93°C (or 180°F/82°C, if your oven goes that low).

3. Choose a pot or Dutch oven in which the steaks will fit snugly; ideally it will be taller than it is wide. Rinse the steaks with cold water and pat dry with paper towels.

4. Bring the fat up to 180°F/82°C over medium heat. Submerge the pork steaks in the fat and transfer the pot, uncovered, to the oven. (Alternatively, you can lower the heat to maintain that temperature and continue cooking on the stovetop.) Cook until tender, 4 to 5 hours.

5. Allow to cool, then refrigerate in the fat until thoroughly chilled. Reheat to serve.

YIELD: 6 ENTRÉE PORTIONS OR 12 APPETIZER PORTIONS

Easy Chicken Confit

Chicken confit is easy to make and a great way to have ready-to-heat-and-eat food in the fridge, as individual portions or as components for tacos, omelets, or pizza. Wings can be confited the same way—finish them after they've chilled by deep-frying and you will have some of the best fried chicken you've ever tasted. Use the whole aromatics below, or use the pureed herbs and spices we use for the Turkey Confit (page 174).

4 pounds/2 kilograms whole chicken legs

2 bay leaves

2 tablespoons whole black peppercorns

2 whole cloves

1 large bunch fresh thyme

6 juniper berries

5 tablespoons/75 grams kosher salt

4 garlic cloves, lightly smashed

1 quart/1 liter rendered duck fat, chicken fat, lard, or olive oil

1. Combine the chicken legs and all the aromatics in a zip-top plastic bag. Rub the aromatics into the chicken. Seal and refrigerate for at least 1 day but optimally 3 days.

2. Preheat the oven to 200°F/93°C (or 180°F/82°C, if your oven goes that low).

3. Choose a pot or Dutch oven in which the chicken legs will fit snugly; ideally it will be taller than it is wide. Melt the fat over medium heat.

4. Rinse the chicken with cold water and pat dry with paper towels.

5. When the fat is melted, add the chicken, making sure it is submerged in the fat. If it's not, add more fat. Bring the fat to 180°F/82°C, then transfer the pot, uncovered, to the oven. (Alternatively, you can lower the heat to maintain that temperature and continue cooking on the stovetop.) Cook until the legs sink to the bottom of the pot and the fat is clear, about 4 hours.

6. Cool the chicken in the fat, then store as described on page 165, step 7.

YIELD: 6 ENTRÉE PORTIONS OR 12 APPETIZER PORTIONS

1: The chicken, salted and mixed with aromatic herbs and spices.
2: Cooking the confit at the proper temperature is important. Notice how clear the fat is when the confit is done.

EASY CHICKEN CONFIT THAT HAS BEEN
CRISPED IN A 350°F OVEN.

Turkey Confit

Turkey is one of the most overlooked meats in the American kitchen, reserved for a holiday and then relegated to the deli counter as thinly sliced breast. A spatchcocked turkey on the grill is thing of wonder. Roasted drumsticks are so good I can't keep my hands off them as soon as they're out of the oven. And confit may well be the best way to prepare turkey, certainly the dark meat. Fully cooked, chilled, then reheated, the meat is succulent and deeply flavorful.

It's very difficult to cook a big turkey so that the thighs are done but the breast is not overcooked. So Brian often makes this confit instead of the traditional roasted bird, roasting a whole breast on the bone so that both white meat and dark meat are cooked to their best advantage.

6 pounds/2.75 kilograms turkey legs

4 garlic cloves, lightly smashed

3 tablespoons chopped shallot

1 bunch fresh flat-leaf parsley

1 bunch fresh thyme, stems removed

1 bunch fresh sage

6 tablespoons/ 90 grams kosher salt

20 whole black peppercorns, crushed

1 teaspoon ground allspice

1 quart/1 liter rendered duck fat, lard, and/or olive oil

———

1. Separate the turkey drumsticks from the thighs. With kitchen shears or a heavy knife, make a cut at the base of each drumstick, severing all tough tendons; this allows the meat to ride up on the bone during cooking for a more compact appearance.

2. Combine all the aromatics and seasonings in a small blender or mini food processor and pulverize into a paste. Rub this mixture all over the turkey drumsticks and thighs, place in a zip-top plastic bag, seal, and refrigerate for 1 to 3 days.

3. Preheat the oven to 200°F/93°C (or 180°F/82°C, if your oven goes that low).

4. Choose a pot or Dutch oven in which the turkey will fit snugly; ideally it will be taller than it is wide. Melt the fat over medium heat.

5. Rinse the turkey with cold water and pat dry with paper towels.

6. When the fat is melted, add the turkey, making sure it is submerged in the fat. If it's not, add more fat. Bring the fat to 180°F/82°C, then transfer the pot, uncovered, to the oven. (Alternatively, you can lower the heat to maintain that temperature and continue cooking on the stovetop.) Cook until the turkey is completely tender and has sunk to the bottom of the pot and the fat is clear, 6 to 8 hours.

7. Cool the turkey in the fat, then store as described on page 165, step 7.

YIELD: 6 ENTRÉE PORTIONS OR 12 APPETIZER PORTIONS

Tongue Confit

Tongue is an overlooked item, and one we wish more people would cook with it. It's a very mild cut, so we prefer smoked tongue for flavor. Confiting is a way to make it tender. This truly does preserve the tongue so that it's good for many months in the fridge if completely submerged in the fat. Slice it thin and serve at room temperature as part of a charcuterie board. Slice it for a sandwich on rye with horseradish cream. Include it in a taco with spicy jicama slaw. Or, of course, add it to any of the meat terrines or meat pies in this book as interior garnish. Tongue is typically boiled then peeled (always peel it while warm), but confiting it results in more flavorful meat. It can also be cooked sous vide (160°F/71°C for 24 hours).

1½ quarts/1.5 liters lard, rendered duck fat, or vegetable oil

3 pounds/1.5 kilograms smoked beef or pork tongue

20 whole black peppercorns

6 juniper berries

4 whole cloves

3 bay leaves

1. Preheat the oven to 200°F/93°C (or 180°F/82°C, if your oven goes that low).

2. Choose a pot or Dutch oven in which the tongue will fit snugly; ideally it will be taller than it is wide. Melt the fat over medium heat.

3. When the fat is melted, add the tongue and seasonings, making sure the tongue is submerged in the fat. If it's not, add more fat.

4. Bring the fat to 180°F/82°C, then transfer the pot, uncovered, to the oven. (Alternatively, you can lower the heat to maintain that temperature and continue cooking on the stovetop.) Cook until the tongue is completely tender, 4 to 5 hours.

5. Cool the tongue in the fat, then store as described on page 165, step 7.

6. To serve, remove the tongue from the fat, peel the skin off the tongue and discard, and slice the tongue.

YIELD: ABOUT 2½ POUNDS/1 KILOGRAM

LEFT: Butternut Squash Confit (page 179)
FOREGROUND: Garlic Confit
BACKGROUND: Fennel Confit (page 178)

Garlic Confit

Garlic slowly cooked until it is mild and tender is an excellent all-purpose condiment to have on hand in the fridge. It's delicious to spread on toast or grilled bread, and is especially good with fish. Garlic confit can garnish stews and braises and soups, top pizza, or be used as a component on a charcuterie board. The cooking medium, olive oil, takes on the garlic flavor and becomes an excellent finishing oil as a by-product of the cooking.

2 heads garlic, cloves separated and peeled

2 bay leaves

15 whole black peppercorns

1 to 2 cups/240 to 480 milliliters extra virgin olive oil, as needed

—

1. Combine the garlic cloves, bay leaves, and peppercorns in a small pot. Pour in enough olive oil to cover the cloves.

2. Bring the oil to 160°F/71°C over low heat and cook at that temperature, uncovered, until the garlic is tender, 35 to 40 minutes.

3. Transfer the garlic and oil to an airtight container and store in the refrigerator until ready to use. They should keep for 2 to 3 weeks.

YIELD: 1 CUP/240 MILLILITERS

Onion Confit

Like Garlic Confit, onion cooked slowly until mild and tender is an excellent item to have ready in the fridge. The onions are cut into thick, inviting slices, ready to be added to salads and sandwiches, or you can warm them up to garnish steak, fish, or omelets.

2 pounds/1 kilogram onions, cut into 1-inch/2.5-centimeter slices

6 garlic cloves, peeled

Kosher salt and freshly ground black pepper to taste

2 cups/480 milliliters extra virgin olive oil

1 cup/240 milliliters vegetable oil

—

1. Combine the onions and garlic in a pot, season them with salt and pepper, and let them sit for about 10 minutes to absorb the salt.

2. Cover the onions with the oil. Bring the oil to between 160°F/71°C and 180°F/82°C over low heat and cook the onions at this temperature until tender, 45 to 60 minutes.

3. Strain, reserving the oil for another use. Refrigerate the onions in a jar until ready to use. They should keep for 2 to 3 weeks.

YIELD: 1 QUART/1 LITER

Fennel Confit

Fennel is an excellent vegetable to confit not only because of its flavor but because its sturdy texture stands up to slow cooking. Here olive oil is the fat of choice and, as with the Garlic Confit (page 177) and Onion Confit (page 177), the fennel is simply cooked in oil at a low temperature until it's tender. Like many products in the realm of charcuterie, this confit is not meant to be the main attraction, but rather a component to other dishes—served alongside a pâté (it goes well with seafood terrines), used as a pizza topping, tossed into a salad, or added to a salsa for grilled fish. Reserve the oil in the refrigerator for up to 2 months; it can be reused for other confits or in marinades.

4 fresh fennel bulbs (about 2 pounds/
1 kilogram total), fronds and outer
leaves removed

8 garlic cloves, lightly smashed

20 whole black peppercorns

Grated zest of 2 oranges

6 cups/1.5 liters extra virgin olive oil

1. Preheat the oven to 200°F/93°C (or 180°F/82°C, if your oven goes that low).

2. Trim any brown off the fennel bulbs and, leaving the root intact, cut each bulb into 8 wedges.

3. Combine the fennel with the remaining ingredients in a tall, narrow pot so that the fennel is submerged. Bring the oil to between 160°F/71°C and 180°F/82°C over medium heat.

4. Transfer the pot to the oven and cook, uncovered, until tender, about 2½ hours.

5. Cool to room temperature, then transfer the fennel and oil to an airtight container and store in the refrigerator for up to 2 months.

YIELD: 8 PORTIONS

Butternut Squash Confit

This is a dish Brian loves to serve at Thanksgiving, using ingredients of the season. If you find yourself with an abundance of butternut squash in the fall, this is a great way to cook it once and have it on hand for a quickly reheated side dish. You can even prepare it in a microwave (see the Note that follows the recipe). Strictly speaking, this recipe isn't in the traditional charcuterie repertoire, but it's within the tradition of charcuterie in that the way it's cooked—poached very gently in olive oil, then cooled—preserves it. Submerged in the olive oil, the squash will keep, refrigerated, for several weeks.

1 (1-pound/450-gram) butternut squash, peeled, seeded, and cut into 1½-inch/4-centimeter dice

2 tablespoons/30 grams kosher salt

2 tablespoons light brown sugar

4 garlic cloves, lightly smashed

Leaves from 1 bunch fresh sage, cut into chiffonade

2 cups/480 milliliters extra virgin olive oil, as needed

¼ cup chopped hazelnuts, toasted

2 tablespoons finely sliced fresh chives

3 tablespoons crumbled goat cheese

1. Spread out the squash on a rimmed baking sheet. Sprinkle the salt and sugar evenly over the squash and let stand for 30 minutes at room temperature.

2. Rinse the squash and pat it dry with paper towels. Put it in a pot that is taller than it is wide. Add the garlic and sage and pour in enough olive oil to cover the squash.

3. Bring the oil to 150°F/65°C over low heat and cook at that temperature, uncovered, until the squash is tender, 45 to 75 minutes. Remove the pot from the heat and serve the squash immediately, using a perforated spoon to allow the oil to drain, or cool the pot, cover, and then refrigerate. If you refrigerate the squash, bring the oil back up to 150°F/65°C over medium-low heat before serving.

4. Serve warm, topped with the hazelnuts, chives, and goat cheese.

YIELD: 6 SIDE-DISH PORTIONS

NOTE: To prepare this in a microwave, salt and rinse the squash as directed, then put it in a large mason jar or tall, narrow microwavable container and add the garlic and sage. Pour in enough olive oil to cover the squash and cook on low (about 20 percent power) for 15 to 20 minutes, until tender. You can reheat it in the microwave as well.

Rillettes

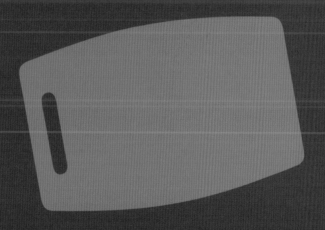

Brian was talking with his friend and fellow chef Ed Janos, both of them deeply experienced in classic cuisine, and Brian told him about the book we were working on. When he heard that rillettes were part of the title, Chef Janos said, "How much is there to say about rillettes?"

Brian told me this laughing because Janos was, in a way, exactly right. Rillettes are so simple and basic as to defy saying more than a sentence or two about them. Pork is braised or confited until it is falling-apart tender, then stirred or paddled with some of the braising liquid and fat and some seasonings. And that's it. Put it in a bowl and scoop it onto crusty bread or crouton and enjoy.

End of introductory material in the chapter, followed by a recipe for classic rillettes, and you're done. What more *is* there to say?

A few things, in fact: Rillettes is a technique and, I might even go so far as to say, a notion, as much as a single preparation. That preparation can be described as above, with classic rillettes often referred to along with the Loire valley town they are associated with: *Le Mans Rillettes de Porc*. But they are also an idea, since most any meat can be cooked low and slow until it's falling-apart tender, and treated as the pork in Le Mans is: duck, rabbit, even chicken. What about lamb? You could braise lamb shanks and create rillettes, but there is a likely reason you don't see this, and it's instructive: Fat is a critical part of rillettes, and cold lamb fat isn't appealing. Nor is beef fat, which is hard at room temperature. Fat is part of what makes good rillettes so appetizing, so we make rillettes from the meats whose fat is so delightful: pork and duck and goose. Rabbit rillettes are also a delight, but they need to be augmented with some tasty pork fat.

Fish also make great rillettes. Salmon and whitefish work particularly well, but we augment them with another delicious fat that's spreadable: butter. All fats are great carriers of flavor.

Rillettes are also considered a preserved meat—often called a potted meat, a meat put up in a pot (or jar). Properly prepared and sealed with a layer of fat, well-made rillettes will indeed keep for several weeks. (Salmon rillettes made with butter will not keep for that long, which is why they are not a traditional confit, but rather a more modern interpretation of them.)

The final component to rillettes is texture. Rillettes can be perfectly smooth and spreadable, or they can be shredded for a coarser texture, or you can leave some of the meat in chunks—it's all up to you. And like a pâté, you can add interior garnish, if you wish, though it's not traditional. Nuts or dried fruit can add textural, flavor, and visual contrasts, or try fresh herbs for visual appeal and a bright flavor.

Excellent cooking is to a large extent about creating flavor. Pork simply braised with salt is porky, but served at room temperature it's a little bland, especially when it's got so much fat that doesn't have a lot of flavor on its own. So we need to introduce powerful flavors to a dish that won't be served hot. And we begin at the beginning, cooking the meat with spices (allspice, cloves, pepper) and aromatics (leek, bay leaf, thyme, garlic, onion). And we cook it, ideally but probably not traditionally, in chicken stock, though you should feel free to use water, which would have been traditional, and wine if you wish. That is flavor. The fat that renders out of the pork shoulder will carry all the spice flavors, and the liquid will pull out the flavor of the aromatics that will ultimately be discarded. Both this flavorful fat and liquid will eventually be all bound up with the shredded meat so that we have an intensely flavored, very rich pot of rillettes.

So this is how we think when we think about rillettes: meat that has a flavorful fat cooked until it's shreddable to spreadable and powerfully seasoned. What follows is the classic pork rillettes preparation, followed by the method for how to turn a confit into rillettes, and finally a variety of contemporary rillettes recipes.

We mean no disrespect to Chef Janos, of course, but there is in fact much to say about rillettes.

Le Mans Rillettes de Porc

There are infinite variations on the classic rillettes, but they all share the fact that fat plays a critical role in the dish. The meat must be cooked in fat until it falls apart, always very slowly to avoid drying it out. The meat is then shredded and mixed with the fat to enrich it and make it spreadable. Serve these rillettes at room temperature with toasted slices of baguette or toast points and traditional accompaniments, such as cornichons and mustard. Like a lot of French classics—béarnaise sauce, for instance, or potatoes lyonnaise—rillettes are named for the place they are associated with: Le Mans, in the Loire valley. And this is why Sancerre, a white or rosé from the Loire, is often a suggested pairing for rillettes, rather than a red wine.

This is a fabulous dish to make during the fall holidays, and it also makes a great gift to bring to friends.

2 pounds/1 kilogram grams fatty pork shoulder (or 1½ pounds/680 grams pork shoulder plus 8 ounces/225 grams pork belly), cut into large (4- to 5-inch/10- to 12-centimeter) chunks

5 garlic cloves, lightly smashed

½ large onion, studded with 6 whole cloves

3 tablespoons/45 grams kosher salt

18 whole black peppercorns

5 allspice berries

1 leek, halved lengthwise

2 bay leaves

1 bunch fresh thyme

1½ cups/360 milliliters chicken stock or water

½ cup/120 milliliters lard

1. Preheat the oven to 275°F/135°C.

2. Combine the pork, garlic, onion, and salt in a thick-bottomed pot or Dutch oven.

3. Make a sachet d'épices by enclosing the peppercorns and allspice berries in a coffee filter or piece of cheesecloth and tying it closed with kitchen string. Make a bouquet garni by tying the leek, bay leaves, and thyme sprigs together with kitchen string. Add these to the pot. Pour the stock over all.

4. Bring the liquid to a boil over high heat, cover, and transfer to the oven. Cook until all the liquid is gone and the meat is very tender and swimming in rendered fat, 5 to 6 hours.

RECIPE CONTINUES ↷

5. Remove and discard the sachet d'épices, bouquet garni, and clove-studded onion. Strain the meat from the liquid, reserving the liquid. Shred the meat with two forks. Put it in the bowl of a standing mixer fitted with a paddle.

6. With the mixer running on low, slowly pour in the cooking liquid until the mixture looks spreadable, then increase the speed to medium and continue to paddle the mixture until smooth. Use all the cooking liquid unless you feel that it looks too soupy (remember that it is gelatinous and will set up when refrigerated).

7. Taste the mixture for seasoning and adjust if necessary. It should taste slightly heavy on the salt if it's still warm, since food served at room temperature (or cold) will need higher seasoning. Pack the meat tightly into a bowl or soufflé dish. Refrigerate until chilled.

8. Melt the lard and pour it over the top of the rillettes so that an even coating of fat covers the surface. Chill until the lard is set.

9. Remove the rillettes from the refrigerator several hours before serving. Properly stored and completely sealed with the fat, rillettes will keep for up to a month in the refrigerator.

YIELD: 8 TO 10 APPETIZER PORTIONS

Rillettes from Any Confit

Traditionally, rillettes are made in the style of the Le Mans Rillettes de Porc (page 185), which calls for meat poached in stock with abundant seasoning. But there are all kinds of good reasons to make rillettes from confit, especially if you keep confit on hand. If you have confit, it means you can have rillettes ready at a moment's notice. If you find yourself with unexpected company, you have what is virtually a ready-made hors d'oeuvres. If you need to supplement a meal, look no further: A salad, a baguette, duck or pork rillettes, and a glass of wine make a fine weekday supper. And, as many of the terrine recipes attest, they're a great garnish in pâtés.

We use duck confit here, but it could be pork, goose, turkey, or chicken. The method is simple: Remove the meat from the bones, if there are any, and paddle it with the fat until it's spreadable. Season to taste. That's it.

If you want to keep the rillettes for many weeks, take an extra step. Pack it tightly into a crock, ramekin, or bowl—air is the enemy here, so make sure there are no air pockets—and chill it, then pour a layer of rendered duck or pork fat over the top so that the meat is completely locked in. Cover it with plastic wrap to prevent it from absorbing other odors and as a further preservative step. Rillettes prepared this way should keep for six weeks or even longer in the fridge.

4 legs Duck Confit (about 1 pound/ 450 grams; page 163)

2 cups/480 milliliters confit cooking fat

Kosher salt and freshly ground black pepper to taste

1. Combine the confit and fat in a large saucepan and heat it over medium heat until the fat is melted and the meat is warmed all the way through.

2. Remove the legs from the fat. Pull off the skin and chop it finely. Pick the meat off the bones, discarding the bones and any tendons and cartilage.

3. Combine the meat and chopped skin in a standing mixer fitted with a paddle. With the machine running on low, add half of the warm fat. Continue to paddle until the mixture has reached a spreadable consistency. (This can also be done by hand using a sturdy wooden spoon. Alternatively, you can puree the meat in a food processor, adding the fat through the feed tube while the machine is running, which will result in a very smooth consistency.) Taste for seasoning, and adjust with salt and pepper as necessary.

4. Fill several ramekins or a soufflé dish ¼ inch/6 millimeters from the top. Chill the rillettes in the fridge until they're cold. Rewarm the remaining fat so that it's pourable and pour it over the rillettes to seal them. Cover and return to the refrigerator until the fat is set. Remove the rillettes from the refrigerator several hours before serving. Properly stored and completely sealed with the fat, rillettes will keep for up to a month in the refrigerator.

YIELD: 6 TO 10 APPETIZER PORTIONS

Rillettes en Terrine

Rillettes are typically served as a potted meat that can be spread with a knife. But if you want to serve them as an individual course, as you might a pâté, you can pack them into a terrine mold. Slice and serve with pickled vegetables and mustard.

2 legs Duck Confit (about 8 ounces/ 225 grams; page 163)

8 ounces/225 grams confit cooking fat

Kosher salt and freshly ground black pepper to taste

1. Combine the confit and fat in a saucepan and heat it over medium heat until the fat is melted and the meat is warmed all the way through.

2. Remove the legs from the fat. Pull off the skin and chop it finely. Pick the meat off the bones, discarding the bones and any tendons and cartilage.

3. Combine the meat and chopped skin in a standing mixer fitted with a paddle. With the machine running on low, add half of the warm fat. Continue to paddle until the mixture has reached a spreadable consistency. (This can also be done by hand using a sturdy wooden spoon. Alternatively, you can puree the meat in a food processor, adding the fat through the feed tube while the machine is running, which will result in a very smooth consistency.) Taste for seasoning, and adjust with salt and pepper as necessary.

4. Line a 2-cup/480-milliliter terrine mold with plastic wrap and fill it with the rillettes. Fold the plastic wrap over the top. Weight the terrine (see page 30) and refrigerate until thoroughly chilled. Unmold, slice, and serve (see page 30). Store leftovers in the refrigerator; properly stored and completely sealed with the fat, rillettes will keep for up to a month.

YIELD: 8 APPETIZER PORTIONS

Rabbit Rillettes

We love to cook with rabbit, and it makes beautiful rillettes. You can poach it in chicken stock, but if you are able to get (or make) veal stock, preferably white veal stock, that gelatin-rich elixir will put these rillettes over the top, bringing depth and soul to the lean meat. If you're a game hunter and get a wild hare, the long cooking technique will work beautifully with that tough, sinewy, deep red meat.

Serve simply on crusty bread or grilled or toasted baguette, perhaps with a little whole-grain mustard (to make your own, see page 228).

1 (1½-pound/680-gram) fresh rabbit, cut into 6 pieces

1 medium leek, halved lengthwise

1 small onion, studded with 3 whole cloves

1 celery stalk

1 small bunch fresh thyme

4 bay leaves

2 tablespoons/30 grams kosher salt

12 whole black peppercorns

5 cups/1.2 liters white veal or chicken stock, or more as needed

1 cup/240 milliliters rendered duck fat or lard, as needed

1. Combine the rabbit and all the aromatics in a pot and pour in the stock. Make sure that all the rabbit pieces are submerged by a good 2 inches/5 centimeters. Bring the stock to a simmer and cook, uncovered, until very tender, 2 to 3 hours.

2. Transfer the rabbit pieces to a plate and strain the stock through a chinois or fine-mesh strainer. When the meat is cool enough to handle but still warm, pick the meat from the bones and put it in a standing mixer fitted with a paddle attachment. Mix on low, adding enough strained stock so that the meat forms a paste. Taste it and add more salt and pepper as needed. Paddle on high for 2 to 3 minutes.

3. Spoon the rabbit mixture into individual ramekins or crocks, filling them ⅛ inch/2.5 millimeters from the top. Refrigerate until chilled. Top with a thin layer of rendered fat, then cover with plastic wrap and return to the refrigerator until the fat has set. Remove the rillettes from the refrigerator at least 2 hours before serving. Store leftovers in the refrigerator for up to 2 weeks.

YIELD: 8 APPETIZER PORTIONS

Wild Atlantic Salmon Rillettes
with Dill and Shallot

Rillettes are traditionally made from poached or confited meat, but the same technique of cooking and combining meat with fat makes these salmon rillettes a delicious hors d'oeuvre. It's a smart way to use scraps of smoked salmon, which gives the rillettes a deeper flavor, but this is optional. Any moderately fatty fish will work here, such as trout or arctic char; wild-caught fish almost always tastes better than farm-raised, so buy that if possible. The ratio of butter and cream is important for a luxurious texture. Serve with crusty bread or water crackers.

½ cup/115 grams unsalted butter

2 tablespoons minced shallot

6 ounces/170 grams fresh salmon trim

2 ounces/60 grams smoked salmon trim or additional fresh salmon

¼ cup/60 milliliters dry white wine

¼ cup/60 milliliters heavy cream

2 tablespoons chopped fresh dill

1 teaspoon/5 grams kosher salt, plus more as needed

½ teaspoon ground white pepper, plus more as needed

1. Melt the butter in a sauté pan over medium heat and add the shallot. Cook until soft but not brown, 30 to 60 seconds. Add the salmon and sauté for 2 minutes. Add the wine, cream, dill, salt, and pepper and simmer for 12 to 15 minutes.

2. Remove the pan from the heat and allow to cool to room temperature. Transfer to a mixer fitted with a paddle attachment. Mix on medium speed until the texture is spreadable, 3 to 4 minutes. Taste for seasoning and add more salt and pepper as needed.

3. Transfer to a serving crock or container, cover, and refrigerate until completely chilled. Remove the rillettes from the refrigerator at least 1 hour before serving. Store leftovers in the refrigerator for up to 4 days.

YIELD: 8 APPETIZER PORTIONS

Smoked Great Lakes Whitefish Rillettes

Because fish don't have abundant fat, to create rillettes with them we need to add fat. With the Wild Atlantic Salmon Rillettes (page 190), it's rich butter and cream. Here it's mayonnaise, seasoned with mustard, dill, and lemon juice. It makes a splendid spread for crackers or toasted baguette slices.

1 pound/450 grams cleaned smoked whitefish

1 cup/240 milliliters mayonnaise

1 tablespoon Dijon mustard

1 tablespoon chopped fresh dill

Juice of 1 lemon

Kosher salt and freshly ground black pepper to taste

Combine the whitefish, mayonnaise, mustard, dill, and lemon juice in a food processor and puree until combined but still a little chunky. Season with salt and pepper and serve. Leftovers will keep, refrigerated, for about a week.

YIELD: 8 APPETIZER PORTIONS

Fennel Rillettes
with Orange and Black Pepper

These modern, nontraditional rillettes are delicious on a cracker, or they could be used to top a canapé, as Brian does with the Cauliflower Mousse (page 110). But they also make a fantastic addition to hot food—Brian tops pizza with fennel rillettes, and he's also used them in place of a meat sauce when making lasagna for his vegetarian sister. Consider adding diced roasted tomato or caramelized eggplant for a flavor variation. These rillettes can be served immediately or refrigerated until ready to use.

1 recipe Fennel Confit (page 178)

1 cup/120 grams finely diced onion

Grated zest of 1 orange

1 tablespoon freshly ground black pepper

1. Heat a bit of the confit oil in a saucepan over medium heat and gently cook the fennel confit just to warm it through. Remove the fennel and dice it small; transfer to a food processor.

2. In the same pan, sauté the onion until very soft. Add it to the food processor, along with the orange zest and black pepper, and puree until smooth.

3. Store in an airtight container in the refrigerator for up to 1 month. It's best if allowed to come to room temperature before serving.

YIELD: 8 APPETIZER PORTIONS

Chanterelle and Garlic Confit Rillettes

We love wild mushrooms and are always looking for ways to prepare them that go beyond sautéing them with shallots and wine and finishing with butter and cream, heavenly though that always is. Here we serve them as rillettes. Brian began making these to use up trim from mushroom dishes at the restaurant, using fragments or less-than-pretty specimens that still taste great. They're fabulous and really feature the earthiness of the mushroom. This technique will, of course, work with cultivated mushrooms as well—use a variety if possible. These make a good side dish for grilled steaks or roasted meats. As with all these nontraditional rillettes, they can be served immediately or refrigerated until ready to use.

1 cup/225 grams unsalted butter, cubed, at room temperature

12 ounces/340 grams chanterelles or other mushrooms, coarsely chopped

Kosher salt and freshly ground black pepper to taste

2 tablespoons minced shallot

½ cup/120 milliliters dry sherry

½ recipe Garlic Confit (page 177)

2 tablespoons fresh lemon juice, plus more as needed

1 teaspoon grated lemon zest

¼ cup chopped fresh flat-leaf parsley

1. Melt half of the butter in a thick-bottomed sauté pan over medium heat. Add the mushrooms and stir, seasoning with salt and pepper. Add the shallot and cook until the water evaporates and the mushrooms start to brown, a few minutes.

2. Deglaze with the sherry. Add the garlic and lemon juice and cook until the water has cooked off and the mushrooms and pan are dry. Remove from the heat and let cool.

3. Combine the cooled mushrooms with the remaining butter, lemon zest, and parsley in a food processor and puree until smooth.

4. Taste and adjust the seasonings with salt, pepper, and lemon juice as necessary, and puree again to distribute the seasoning.

YIELD: 8 APPETIZER PORTIONS

Charcuterie Specialties

We love pâtés, confits, and rillettes, but the collection of recipes in this chapter shows a range of forcemeat techniques and other uses of the pig that fall within charcuterie's purview, such as Porchetta di Testa (page 205), crispy pig skin, and several different pork belly creations (because who doesn't want more pork belly when given the option?).

There are classic pâtés here, but because they are cooked in unique ways, outside a terrine, we've put them in this chapter. Stuffed duck neck uses the skin of the duck's neck like a large sausage casing. It's a preparation that reminds us that this specialty demands versatility and total use of the animal; here, the duck neck skin is as valuable as the duck breast. It's visually stunning and, when roasted until the duck skin is crispy, enormously gratifying to eat. All of charcuterie is about the odd bits, the stuff that might otherwise be thrown away but, when used, can result in an extra meal.

Brian likes to remind me that the galantine (poached pâté, served cold) and the ballotine (roasted pâté, served hot) were important dishes two hundred years ago, and even earlier. They're projects for the home cook—they're simply not practical for restaurant chefs doing a high volume—yet we still believe that they remain important dishes. The chicken galantine in our first book together, *Charcuterie*, is so good that Brian has every class he teaches make one. I've made it several times and I agree—it's a preparation that's more than worth the effort, and worthy of being revived. Here we do a Seafood Galantine (page 218) and a Turkey Ballotine (page 216). We also have Ham and Parsley en Gelée (page 212), which is a classic preparation that's finished in a terrine mold, but we put it here because it seems a one-of-a-kind dish. The first time Brian saw this dish, it was being demonstrated by Jacques Pépin, a classic in his own right. And we are also including here another classic we would like to see on more menus and kitchen tables, Chicken Quenelles (page 214).

We have pork preparations that we love, such as Cracklings (page 221), Puffy Chicharrón (page 220), and traditional Rillons (crispy chunks of pork belly that can be eaten hot or cold; page 219). And finally, two additional pork belly preparations with Asian spices—one braised and tender (page 222), one crispy (page 223)—because there are few things more satisfying than crispy pork belly.

And we include two preparations for the pig's head, which is composed of all kinds of deliciousness if you know how to get at it—ears and cheeks and skin. This is real cooking. This is transformative cooking—craftsmanship that transforms difficult cuts into great food and likewise transforms the cook who does this very special work.

Crispy Stuffed Duck Neck

Back in the 1980s, when Brian was a chef at the Lark in Detroit, the owner asked him to put more "country-style" dishes on the menu. This, after some research, was one of the dishes he came up with. True to peasant cuisine, it uses the neck skin of the duck as well as the gizzards and heart. Such cooking wouldn't discard anything; it would put all of the animal to use. The neck skins serve as the casings for a pork pâté with abundant garnish, and served hot, as individual ballotines. Whole ducks, like rabbit, are increasingly available at growers' markets. These would be the best place to source duck necks.

If you have a smoker, Brian suggests cold-smoking the necks for 2 to 3 hours after they've been poached and before roasting, for additional flavor.

5 ounces/140 grams duck or chicken gizzards and hearts, cut into ½-inch/1-centimeter pieces

½ teaspoon pink curing salt

1 teaspoon grated nutmeg

Pinch ground white pepper, optional

6 tablespoons/90 milliliters rendered duck fat, bacon fat, lard, or unsalted butter

1½ pounds/680 grams onions, thinly sliced

3 garlic cloves, minced

¼ cup/60 milliliters port

1½ cups/360 milliliters chicken stock

1 pound/450 grams pork shoulder, cut into 1-inch/2.5-centimeter dice

1 pound/450 grams pork belly, cut into 1-inch/2.5-centimeter dice

1 tablespoon/15 grams kosher salt

½ teaspoon coarsely ground black pepper

8 ounces/225 grams ham, cut into ½-inch/1-centimeter dice

⅓ cup/30 grams shelled pistachios, blanched

8 duck necks

RECIPE CONTINUES ↻

1. Toss the gizzards and hearts in a nonreactive bowl with the pink salt, nutmeg, and white pepper (if using). Cover and refrigerate for 12 to 24 hours.

2. Melt the fat in a thick-bottomed sauté pan over medium-high heat and add the onions and garlic. Rinse the gizzards and hearts under cold water, pat them dry, and add them to the pan. Sauté until the onions are soft and beginning to turn light brown, then deglaze with the port. Add the chicken stock and simmer until the gizzards and hearts are tender, 45 minutes to 1 hour. Transfer the gizzards and hearts to a plate, cover, and chill. Increase the heat to medium-high and reduce any liquid remaining in the onions to a syrup consistency. Refrigerate until chilled.

3. In a bowl, combine the pork shoulder and pork belly. Add the chilled onions and reduced liquid, as well as the kosher salt and black pepper. Grind it all through a ⅛ inch/3-millimeter die into the bowl of a standing mixer set in an ice bath. Fit the bowl into the standing mixer and, using the paddle attachment, mix at medium speed for 1 to 2 minutes. Sauté a tablespoon of the mixture and taste it for seasoning, then adjust as necessary. Add the gizzards, hearts, ham, and pistachios. Paddle for another minute.

4. Carefully remove the skin from the duck necks (reserve the bones for stock). Turn the skins inside out and scrape them clean of all fat and any glands that may still be attached, then turn them right side out again. Tie off the smaller end of each duck neck skin. Pipe or stuff the ground meat and garnish mixture into the neck skin. Fill the neck full without breaking it, then sew or tie off the other end to close the stuffed neck.

5. Bring a large pot of water to 170°F/76°C and poach the stuffed necks until the internal temperature reaches 150°F/65°C, 20 to 40 minutes, depending on the size of the necks. Cool the stuffed necks in their poaching liquid. Meanwhile, preheat the oven to 425°F/218°C.

6. Remove the necks from the poaching liquid and lay them in a roasting pan. Roast until hot all the way through, about 20 minutes, and serve hot.

YIELD: 8 ENTRÉE PORTIONS

CRISPY STUFFED DUCK NECK
(PAGE 199)

Fromage de Tête

This is one of the easiest and most traditional (not to mention tastiest) ways to use the abundance of edibles contained in a pig's head. Most cultures have some version of it. In England it's called brawn, and in Italy it's soppressata di Toscano (throughout the rest of Italy, soppressata refers to a dry-cured sausage). The French name, which translates as headcheese, strikes us as one of the more unfortunate terms in the charcutier's nomenclature. But there it is. And regardless of what it's called, all these preparations are the same: A whole pig's head is submerged in water with lots of aromatics and cooked until it's falling-apart tender. Everything edible is then picked from the head and diced as appropriate, packed with herbs into a terrine, and covered with poaching liquid, which should be very gelatinous. Brian likes to add more gelatin just to be sure it all sets up. For a different dish altogether, you can increase the amount of gelatin by half, cut the terrine into 1-inch/2.5-centimeter slices, then bread and pan-fry them. Served with a warm mustard vinaigrette, it's a knockout.

Serve with Sauce Gribiche (page 230), and an arugula salad topped with herbed vinaigrette alongside.

1 fresh pig's head, on the bone, ears and tongue included (sizes vary; usually about 16 pounds/7 kilograms)

Kosher salt as needed

2 cups/480 milliliters dry white wine

1 leek, halved lengthwise

2 bay leaves

1 bunch fresh thyme

1 bunch fresh flat-leaf parsley, plus ½ cup chopped fresh flat-leaf parsley

4 garlic cloves, lightly smashed

15 whole black peppercorns

10 whole cloves

5 allspice berries

2 tablespoons powdered gelatin

¼ cup champagne vinegar

1. Place the pig's head in a large pot and, using a large liquid measuring cup, cover it completely with cold water, keeping track of how much water you use. Remove the head. Add kosher salt to the water at a ratio of 1 cup/240 grams per 1 gallon/3.75 liters.

2. Place the head in the salted water and soak for 12 hours or overnight (preferably in the refrigerator, but if you don't have space, place it in the coolest spot available).

3. Drain the pig's head and return it to the pot. Cover with fresh water by at least 2 inches/5 centimeters. Add the wine.

4. Make a bouquet garni by tying the leek, bay leaves, thyme sprigs, and parsley sprigs together with kitchen string. Make a sachet d'épices by enclosing the garlic cloves, peppercorns, cloves, and allspice berries in a coffee filter or piece of cheesecloth and tying it closed with kitchen string. Add these to the pot. Bring to a simmer and gently poach until all the meat is completely tender and falling off the bone, 2½ to 3 hours.

5. Remove the head from the broth; when it is cool enough to handle, pull off all the meat, including the tongue and ears. Cut the meat into ½-inch/1-centimeter pieces and set aside in a bowl; discard the head. Strain the broth through a chinois lined with cheesecloth and cool to room temperature.

6. Pour ½ cup/120 milliliters cold water into a small saucepan and sprinkle the gelatin over it. Let it sit for 3 to 4 minutes to bloom (that is, absorb the water without forming clumps). Add 2 cups/480 milliliters of the strained poaching liquid and heat gently to dissolve. Remove the pan from the heat and add the vinegar.

7. Add the chopped parsley to the bowl of meat, and moisten the meat with the gelatin mixture, enough to facilitate uniform mixing; toss gently.

8. Line a 1½-quart/1.5-liter terrine mold with plastic wrap and fill it with the meat mixture. Pour the remaining gelatin mixture over the meat just to cover (this will ensure that everything is properly bound), then fold the plastic wrap over the top, pressing down to make sure all the ingredients are covered. Refrigerate overnight, or for up to a week. Unmold, slice, and serve (see page 30).

YIELD: 12 APPETIZER PORTIONS

PORCHETTA DI TESTA

Porchetta di Testa

Working with a fresh pig's head can be dead simple, as in the Fromage de Tête (page 202), or fairly tricky, as here. In this quintessential Italian peasant preparation, the idea is to combine all the various cuts of a pig's head—cheeks and ears and jowl and snout and skin—season it all thoughtfully, wrap it up into a bundle, cook it low and slow until it's completely tender, chill it, then slice it very, very thin and serve it cold with a Sauce Gribiche (page 230) or a vinaigrette. It can also be cut into thicker slices, breaded with panko, and pan-fried for a completely different but equally delicious preparation.

Depending on the size of the head, you can roll the entire thing or split it in half to make two smaller rolls. Rolling the whole head will give you an oval with a diameter of 6 to 8 inches/15 to 20 centimeters.

The time-consuming part of this is boning the pig's head. If you're a cook familiar with tricky bones, like lamb shoulder, you can figure it out. If it's your first time, be patient because the skull is tricky. Furthermore, different slaughterhouses cut differently, leaving more or less jowl on the head. Sometimes most of the flesh is removed from around the eyes, leaving gaping holes there. Regardless of either of those issues, this recipe is a standard for all Brian's charcuterie boards and can be adjusted up or down without a problem. Always use the ears and tongue (smoke the tongue if you're able). Often there will be hair left on the face, especially around the ears. Wash the head well, dry it, then use a disposable shaver to clean up any residual stubble, or burn it off with a brûlée torch. And be on the lookout for and remove any glands, the brownish soft pieces embedded in the fat.

If you have sous vide capacity, we recommend this method for perfect doneness and texture (see the Note below the recipe). If not, the old-fashioned roasting method always works.

1 pig's head, on the bone, ears and tongue attached or reserved (sizes vary; usually about 16 pounds/7 kilograms)

FOR EVERY 3½ POUNDS/1.5 KILOGRAMS, YOU WILL NEED THE FOLLOWING SEASONINGS:

¼ teaspoon pink curing salt, optional

1 tablespoon/15 grams kosher salt

2 tablespoons freshly ground black pepper

2 tablespoons fennel seeds, toasted

2 tablespoons grated orange zest

2 tablespoons grated lemon zest

2 tablespoons minced garlic

RECIPE CONTINUES ➔

1. Preheat the oven to 275°F/135°C.

2. Turn the pig's head upside down and, starting at the chin, cut away all fat and meat, keeping your knife as close to the bone as possible; be sure to capture the cheek meat. Remove the meat, skin, and fat in one piece if possible. Remove the ears and tongue if they have not already been separated from the head; reserve (smoke the tongue if you can).

3. With the skin side down, remove all glands and discard.

4. Sprinkle with the pink salt (if using), then sprinkle the kosher salt all over the flesh. Evenly distribute all the other seasonings.

5. Lay the ears in the center, then the tongue. Roll the face around the tongue and ears, shaping it into a log. Tie securely with butcher's twine.

6. Wrap the head tightly in parchment paper, twisting both ends to compact the head, then wrap it tightly in aluminum foil. Place it on a rimmed baking sheet and roast until completely tender, 6 to 8 hours. Transfer the wrapped head to an ice bath to chill for 30 minutes, then refrigerate for at least 12 hours and up to 1 month.

7. To serve, unwrap and slice paper-thin using a deli meat slicer (or an extremely sharp, thin-bladed slicing knife), lay thin slices on a plate as if it were beef carpaccio, and serve cold.

YIELD: 36 APPETIZER PORTIONS

NOTE: To cook the pig's head sous vide, set your immersion circulator and water bath for 160°F/71°C. Seal the head in plastic for sous viding, making sure there are no air pockets. Submerge the head in the water bath for 36 hours. Transfer to an ice bath to chill for 30 minutes, then refrigerate for at least 12 hours and up to 1 month.

Salo (Slovakian Cured Fat)

Brian wanted to offer an Eastern European version of dry-cured back fat to demonstrate that Italians aren't the only people to serve it. Slovakian cured back fat, with or without skin, is often treated with paprika as we do here. Southern Slovakian people usually smoke their back fat, so these variations of lardo are much more highly flavored than the Italian version. Slice this thin and serve, or include it as part of a charcuterie board.

1 (2-pound/1-kilogram) slab pork back fat, about 15 by 20 inches/40 by 50 centimeters and 1 inch/2.5 centimeters thick

Paprika as needed

2 pounds/1 kilogram salt

12 garlic cloves, lightly smashed

¼ cup whole black peppercorns

1. Dust the fat with paprika, evenly covering the entire surface.

2. Combine the salt with the garlic and peppercorns. Spread a layer of the salt mixture in the bottom of a nonreactive container just large enough to hold the fat, place the fat on top, and cover completely with the remaining salt mixture. Cover with plastic wrap and refrigerate for 3 months. Brush off the salt with a dry cloth before serving.

YIELD: 24 APPETIZER PORTIONS

ROAST SADDLE OF RABBIT WITH
SPINACH AND PINE NUTS, SERVED
WITH CRUSTY BREAD AND RED WINE

Roast Saddle of Rabbit with Spinach and Pine Nuts

One rabbit, with the help of pork and fat and garnishes, can create a wonderful bacon-wrapped roulade that will serve four. The dark meat, ground, serves as the base of the farce, while the midsection of the rabbit, the saddle or loin, is kept whole and used as an inlayed garnish (as opposed to a folded-in garnish, which this preparation also includes: spinach, sweetbreads, and pine nuts). The bones can be roasted and used to make a stock that can be reduced to a sauce for total utilization of the rabbit.

This dish goes well with all the standard condiments.

1 (3-pound/1.5-kilogram) rabbit

6 ounces/170 grams pork back fat, cut into ½-inch/1-centimeter dice

3 ounces/85 grams pork shoulder, cut into ½-inch/1-centimeter dice

1 large egg

½ teaspoon All-Purpose Spice Mix for Meat Pâtés (page 33)

Kosher salt to taste

½ teaspoon ground white pepper

1 cup/30 grams fresh spinach chiffonade

3 ounces/85 grams cooked sweetbreads (see page 65), broken into chunks

¼ cup pine nuts

12 thin slices bacon

1. Preheat the oven to 375°F/190°C.

2. Remove the legs from the rabbit, then remove the meat from the leg bones; set aside. (Reserve the leg bones for stock.)

3. With the carcass lying on its back, carefully remove all the remaining meat in one piece, keeping the knife as close to the bone as possible. (Reserve the carcass for stock.) Remove any fat from the meat and discard. Lay the meat out flat on a piece of plastic wrap. Gently pound the flanks flat without hitting the loins that run down the center.

4. Grind the rabbit leg meat, pork back fat, and pork shoulder through a ⅛-inch/3-millimeter die into a metal bowl set in an ice bath. Transfer the ground meat to a food processor, add the egg, spice mix, salt, and white pepper, and puree until smooth.

5. Do a quenelle test (see page 28) and adjust the seasoning as necessary.

6. Transfer the pâté to a bowl and fold in the spinach, sweetbreads, and pine nuts. Shape the mixture into a log that will fit inside the pounded rabbit. Lay it in the center, between the loins. Smooth the surface and enclose the log in the pounded rabbit, making sure the flanks overlap.

RECIPE CONTINUES ➔

7. Shingle the bacon on a piece of plastic wrap, overlapping the edges slightly. Place the rabbit roulade on the bacon and roll it in the plastic wrap so that the bacon encloses the rabbit. Twist the ends tightly to compact the forcemeat. Remove the plastic wrap and rewrap in a sheet of oiled aluminum foil, again twisting the ends tightly.

8. Place on a rimmed baking sheet and roast to an internal temperature of 145°F/63°C, 25 to 30 minutes.

9. Allow the roulade to rest for 5 to 10 minutes before slicing into ½-inch/1-centimeter disks; serve.

YIELD: 4 ENTRÉE PORTIONS

La Caillette (Rhône Valley Meatballs)

Pronounced "ky-YET," these meatballs hail from Ardèche in south central France in the Rhône Valley, an area famous for chestnuts, sheep, the Rhône River, and the country-style cooking embodied by this dish. These meatballs were traditionally made from scraps on the day of the slaughter and eaten as the main meal when the work was done. Cabbage or Swiss chard is usually used, but these meatballs—which should be rolled large—are always wrapped in caul fat, which bastes the meat and helps retain moisture while cooking. Caul fat can be hard to come by and is more easily found online.

1 pound/450 grams Swiss chard; make sure there are enough large leaves to wrap 12 (3-ounce/85-gram) meatballs

2 tablespoons unsalted butter

2 tablespoons minced shallot

2 tablespoons minced garlic

½ cup/120 milliliters port

1 pound/450 grams pork shoulder, cut into 1-inch/2.5-centimeter pieces

8 ounces/225 grams pork liver, cut into 1-inch/2.5-centimeter pieces

8 ounces/225 grams fresh pork belly or slab bacon, cut into 1-inch/2.5-centimeter pieces

¼ cup chopped fresh flat-leaf parsley

1 large egg

1 tablespoon/15 grams kosher salt

1½ teaspoons freshly ground black pepper

12 (6-inch/15-centimeter) squares of caul fat (see page 137), soaked in cold water

Dry white wine as needed

1. Preheat the oven to 325°F/160°C.

2. Bring a large pot of salted water to a boil and prepare an ice bath. Remove the stems from the Swiss chard and reserve them. Blanch the leaves in the salted water for 30 seconds, then transfer them to the ice bath. When they're chilled, drain and pat dry, keeping the leaves as intact as possible.

3. Mince the chard stems. Melt the butter in a sauté pan and sauté the stems until soft, 30 seconds or so, then add the shallot and garlic. Cook until soft, another minute or two, then deglaze with the port. Set the pan aside to cool.

4. Grind the pork shoulder, pork liver, pork belly, and parsley together through a ¼-inch/6-millimeter die into a metal bowl set in an ice bath. Add the chard-garlic mixture, egg, salt, and pepper to the ground meat and mix well by hand. Form the mixture into 12 meatballs, each about the size of a lemon.

5. Choose an oven-safe vessel that is just big enough for all the meatballs to fit snugly in a single layer. Lay a square of caul on a work surface and place one or two blanched chard leaves on top. Place a meatball on top and enclose it in the chard and caul fat. Press the meatball into the baking dish to flatten it. Repeat with the remaining meatballs.

6. Add enough white wine to go halfway up the meatballs and bake until cooked through, 35 to 40 minutes. Serve warm.

YIELD: 12 APPETIZER PORTIONS

Ham and Parsley en Gelée

With the help of a rich broth, trim (ham) and an inexpensive herb (parsley) combine to make an elegant and satisfying first course. Serve it with a simple mustard vinaigrette. Brian learned this classic dish from Jacques Pépin, and it's an honor to bring it into the spotlight. Jamon de Paris, a beautiful boiled ham, is ideal for this preparation, but any cooked or smoked ham will work.

¾ cup/180 milliliters cold water

1½ tablespoons powdered gelatin

3 cups/720 milliliters rich chicken or pork broth (preferably clarified; see box below)

2 tablespoons/30 grams kosher salt

2 pounds/1 kilogram ham, cut into ½-inch/1-centimeter dice

1 cup/90 grams roughly chopped fresh flat-leaf parsley

1. Pour the cold water into a small bowl and sprinkle the gelatin over it. Let it sit for 3 to 4 minutes to bloom (that is, absorb the water without forming clumps).

2. Bring the broth to a low simmer in a saucepan. Add the salt, then stir in the bloomed gelatin and water. Taste the broth and add more salt if necessary. Remove from the heat and cool to room temperature. Stir in the ham and parsley.

3. Line a 1½-quart/1.5-liter terrine mold with plastic wrap. Pour the ham and parsley mixture into the mold. Fold the plastic wrap over the top. Refrigerate until thoroughly chilled and the gelatin has set. Unmold, slice, and serve (see page 30).

YIELD: 8 APPETIZER PORTIONS

TO CLARIFY BROTH

While this step is not necessary from a flavor standpoint, it makes a big enough difference in the appearance to make it worth the effort.

3 cups/720 milliliters rich chicken or pork broth

3 large egg whites, lightly whisked (just to break them up a bit)

1. Warm the broth on the stove so that it's warm but not too hot to touch.

2. Whisk in the egg whites to distribute.

3. Turn the heat to medium-high and bring to a simmer, stirring continuously with a flat-edged wooden spoon or spatula to keep the egg whites from sticking to the bottom of the pan.

4. As the broth begins to simmer, stop stirring and allow the egg white "raft" to rise to the surface. Lower the heat to a very gentle simmer and cook for 10 to 15 minutes.

5. Using a ladle, transfer the stock to a strainer lined with cheesecloth, picking up as little of the egg white raft as possible. Once all the stock is strained, line the strainer with a coffee filter and strain it again. Refrigerate until ready to use.

YIELD: 2 CUPS/480 MILLILITERS

Chicken Quenelles with Mushroom Cream Sauce

When Brian and I traveled to Lyon to attend the Pâté en Croûte world championship an hour south of that culinary capital, we ate in a few *bouchons*, small bistros that serve a limited traditional menu. The type of restaurant and menu is so specific that the city designates only about twenty that are considered to be *vrais* (true) *bouchons*. One of those menu items is a pike quenelle with some sort of fish velouté, or creamy sauce. Pike is flavorful but impossibly bony, so the fish is pressed through a tamis to separate the bones from the fish for a perfect use of the quenelle technique: Puree meat with cream, egg, and seasonings, then drop spoonfuls of it into simmering liquid until set, and serve with a cream sauce.

Brian uses this technique for all the chicken tenderloins he pulls off the breasts for a sautéed breast preparation. They tend to separate from the breast when cooking, making them problematic in a restaurant situation. He could throw them into a family meal of some sort, but he'd rather make money from them. So, he creates a delicious and satisfying starter course, chicken quenelles speckled with fresh chives and spiced with nutmeg, served in a rich mushroom cream sauce. We think these quenelles are so good that they're worth making on their own, not waiting until you have the trim. These also make for a very elegant garnish in a chicken soup.

FOR THE QUENELLES:

3 cups/720 milliliters chicken stock

Unsalted butter, for greasing the pan

8 ounces/225 grams boneless, skinless chicken breast, cut into 1-inch/2.5-centimeter dice

1 teaspoon/5 grams kosher salt

Freshly ground black pepper to taste

Grated nutmeg to taste

1 large egg white

¾ cup/180 milliliters heavy cream

2 tablespoons minced fresh chives

FOR THE SAUCE:

2 tablespoons unsalted butter

1 tablespoon minced shallot

1 tablespoon minced garlic

1 pound/450 grams assorted mushrooms, thinly sliced

Kosher salt and freshly ground black pepper to taste

½ cup/120 milliliters dry sherry

1 tablespoon all-purpose flour

½ cup/120 milliliters chicken stock

1 cup/240 milliliters heavy cream

2 tablespoons chopped fresh flat-leaf parsley

1. To make the quenelles, warm the chicken stock to 170°F/76°C on the stovetop. Butter a baking pan or other dish that can sit on a burner.

2. Season the chicken with the salt, pepper, and nutmeg. Put it in a food processor with the egg white and puree until smooth. With the machine running, slowly add the cream, scraping down the sides at least once. Transfer the mixture to a bowl and fold in the chives.

3. With two medium-size spoons, shape the mousseline mixture into 12 three-sided dumplings. Gently place the quenelles in the buttered dish. Carefully pour the warm stock into the pan and gently poach the quenelles, never allowing the stock to get above 170°F/76°C, until firm and cooked through, 3 to 5 minutes. Remove the pan from the heat and keep warm.

4. To make the sauce, melt the butter in a sauté pan over medium-high heat. Add the shallot and garlic and sauté until soft. Add the mushrooms and season with salt and pepper. Cook for 5 minutes. Deglaze with the sherry and continue to cook until all the liquid has evaporated. Dust with the flour and cook for 3 minutes. Add the chicken stock, bring to a boil, then add the cream. Season with salt and pepper and cook until the sauce is smooth and creamy, adjusting the consistency with more stock if it gets too thick.

5. To serve, place the quenelles in a serving dish, spoon some sauce over each, and sprinkle with the chopped parsley.

YIELD: 6 APPETIZER PORTIONS

Turkey Ballotine

The term *ballotine* denotes a pâté that is shaped into a roulade, roasted, and served hot. Traditionally, a ballotine is like any other pâté, inlayed down the center with a whole cut of meat, with the skin serving as the casing. Duck Pâté (page 36), for instance, would make a great ballotine. You would lay out a rectangle of duck skin, scraped of its fat, lay a strip of forcemeat down the center, place the duck breasts on top and cover them with the remaining farce, shape it into a roulade, tie it, then roast it on a bed of mirepoix (diced onion, carrot, and celery).

Here, Brian wanted to use as much of the turkey breast, and only the turkey breast, as possible, so he reverses this strategy, pounding out the whole breast and using that to encase a rich farce of pork, pork fat, and turkey tenderloin. For flavor and fat, the breast is wrapped in bacon.

1 (3-pound/1.5-kilogram) whole boneless, skinless turkey breast

1 tablespoon vegetable oil

¼ cup minced shallot

¼ cup minced garlic

¾ cup/180 milliliters dry sherry

4 ounces/110 grams pork back fat, diced

2 ounces/60 grams pork butt, diced

1 large egg white

1 tablespoon/15 grams kosher salt

2 teaspoons freshly ground black pepper

1 teaspoon All-Purpose Spice Mix for Meat Pâtés (page 33)

½ cup/15 grams fresh spinach chiffonade

1 ounce/30 grams dried tart cherries

12 thin slices bacon

———

1. Preheat the oven to 350°F/175°C.

2. Trim the edges of the breast and remove the tenderloins. Clean the meat of all sinew. Weigh out 6 ounces/170 grams of tenderloin and/or lean trim meat and dice it for grinding. (You'll have considerably more than that, so reserve the remaining trim for another use—add to soup; pound flat, coat with panko, and pan-fry; or make quenelles, page 28.)

3. Each breast half is shaped like a triangular lobe, with a thick wide top tapering to a thin point. Butterfly the breast by slicing through the thick part about two-thirds of the way down, using your judgment to create one uniformly thick piece once it's pounded. Place between two pieces of plastic wrap and pound slightly to obtain an even thickness.

4. Heat the vegetable oil in a sauté pan over medium-high heat and sauté the shallot and garlic until translucent, a minute or so. Add the sherry and reduce it to a syrup. Cool to room temperature.

5. Grind the 6 ounces/170 grams of turkey trim with the pork fat and pork butt through a ⅛-inch/3-millimeter die into a metal bowl set in an ice bath. Transfer the mixture to a food processor, add the egg white, salt, pepper, spice mix, and the cooled reduction, and puree until smooth. Transfer the puree to a bowl and fold in the spinach and dried tart cherries.

6. Cut a piece of aluminum foil longer than the length of the turkey breast. Lay the foil out on a work surface. Shingle the bacon slices on the foil.

7. Spread the forcemeat down the center of the turkey breast and roll the breast into a log. Place the log on the center of the bacon slices. Wrap the bacon-lined foil around the turkey. Twist the ends of the foil tightly to compact the turkey.

8. Place the turkey on a rack set over a roasting pan and roast until it reaches an internal temperature of 155°F/68°C, about 1 hour.

9. Let it rest for 20 to 30 minutes, then unwrap, slice, and serve.

YIELD: 12 FIRST-COURSE SERVINGS

Seafood Galantine

Galantine generally refers to one of the basic forcemeats wrapped in its own skin and poached. Here we use a standard all-purpose shrimp mousseline, loaded with spinach and nutmeg, combined with a whole cut of salmon. We roll the two together jellyroll style, seal it in plastic, and poach it as a roulade. This preparation calls for butterflying the salmon, so you need salmon cut closer to the head rather than the tapered tail end. The thickness of the fish and forcemeat are important to ensure even cooking—each should be about ½ inch/1 centimeter thick.

1 pound/450 grams skinless salmon (cut from the thicker, or head side)

6 ounces/170 grams rock shrimp, peeled and deveined

1 large egg white

1 tablespoon/15 grams kosher salt

1 teaspoon ground white pepper

½ teaspoon grated nutmeg

¼ cup/60 milliliters heavy cream

1 cup/30 grams fresh spinach chiffonade

1. Butterfly the salmon, cutting through the thick part of the fillet. Place it between two pieces of plastic wrap and gently pound it to even out the thickness to about ½ inch/1 centimeter. It should be a rectangle of about 8 by 12 inches/20 by 30 centimeters.

2. Combine the shrimp, egg white, and seasonings in a food processor and puree until smooth. With the machine running, slowly add the cream. Transfer to a mixing bowl and fold in the spinach.

3. Lay the salmon fillet, skin side up, on a sheet of plastic wrap much larger than the rectangle of fish. Spread the mousseline evenly over the salmon, about the same thickness as the salmon.

4. Using the plastic wrap, roll the fish into a roulade, tighten by twisting the ends, and tie off the ends. Rewrap the roulade in a second layer of plastic wrap to reinforce the shape, tightening and tying off the ends.

5. Bring a large pot of water to 160°F/71°C and poach the galantine to an internal temperature of 135°F/57°C. Transfer it to an ice bath to chill completely. Refrigerate until ready to serve. Unwrap, slice, and serve.

YIELD: 8 APPETIZER PORTIONS

Rillons (Crispy Pork Belly)

Rillons are pieces of meaty pork belly that have been slowly cooked in a little fat until they caramelize. They're first cooked covered and then again uncovered, and removed from their fat before being refrigerated. Rillons are a great all-purpose meat to eat, hot or cold, for breakfast or lunch or as a component for dinner. Quatre épices (a spice mixture that usually includes four of the following: ground pepper, nutmeg, ginger, cinnamon, cloves) is often used to season, and it's a good starting point. But you can change the spice to achieve the flavor profile you are looking for. While we call for skinned chunks of belly, it is cooked long enough that you can use skin-on belly if you like.

2 pounds/1 kilogram skinless pork belly, cut into 3-inch/8-centimeter cubes

2 tablespoons/30 grams kosher salt

2 teaspoons quatre épices

1½ cups/360 milliliters rendered lard

2 tablespoons sugar

1. Toss the pork cubes with the salt and quatre épices. Cover and refrigerate overnight.

2. Melt the lard in a large skillet over medium heat. Add the meat and brown on all sides, about 15 minutes.

3. Lower the heat and cover the skillet. Cook the meat, stirring the pot every once in a while, for 1½ hours.

4. Remove the lid and sprinkle the sugar over the meat. Turn the heat to medium-high and continue cooking the rillons until they're deeply caramelized and delicious looking, about 20 minutes more.

5. Remove the rillons from the fat. They can be served right away or refrigerated and then served cold, at room temperature, or reheated as you wish.

YIELD: 8 TO 10 APPETIZER PORTIONS

Puffy Chicharrón

Chicharrón are pieces of pork skin that are treated in such a way that, when dropped into hot fat—puff!—they turn light and crispy. There are two steps to making them. Pig skin is a network of connective tissue, collagen, fat, and water. Were you to simply deep-fry pig skin, it wouldn't tenderize. But if you braise the skin until it's tender and then deep-fry it, it pops madly as the water in the skin vaporizes. What you must do is cook it to tenderize it, remove as much fat as possible from the skin, and then dehydrate the skin. Brian believes that an initial step, adding baking soda to the cooking water, also contributes to the crispiness.

Because the initial cooking in water to tenderize the skin also removes most of the flavor, it's important to give flavor back to the skin, with both salt and whatever additional enhancements you wish. Here we suggest a simple dusting of smoked paprika, chili powder, and cumin. But Brian has also dehydrated cheddar cheese, pulverized it, and seasoned the chicharrón with this to simulate our favorite commercial snack food, cheese puffs.

FOR THE SPICE MIXTURE:

¼ cup sweet smoked paprika (preferably pimentón de la Vera)

2 tablespoons sugar

2 tablespoons chili powder

1 tablespoon ground cumin

1 tablespoon freshly ground black pepper

1 tablespoon cayenne pepper

FOR THE CHICHARRÓN:

6 quarts/6 liters water

3 tablespoons baking soda

2 pounds/1 kilogram pork skin, cut into large pieces

Vegetable oil, for deep-frying

Kosher salt to taste

—

1. Mix all the ingredients for the spice mixture until uniformly combined; set aside.

2. Combine the water and baking soda in a large pot. Add the pork skin, bring to a simmer, and cook for 1½ to 2 hours. Drain the skin, then chill it in the refrigerator for at least 2 hours.

3. Lay the skin on a work surface with the outer side down and scrape away the soft, excess fat with a spoon or a bench scraper. Pat the skin dry with paper towels.

4. Dehydrate the skin overnight, either in a dehydrator or in an oven set at 150°F/65°C, until completely hard and brittle. If your oven only goes down to 200°F/93°C, leave the oven door ajar. Break the skin into 1-inch/2.5-centimeter pieces.

5. Pour the oil into a large pot to a depth of about 1½ inches/4 centimeters and bring it to 375°F/190°C. Fry the skin pieces; they should puff immediately and be done in 10 seconds or so. Remove with a skimmer and drain on paper towels.

6. Dust the chicharrón with salt and the spice mixture and serve hot.

YIELD: 12 APPETIZER PORTIONS

Cracklings

Cracklings are simply crispy bits of pork skin. When making that golden elixir known as schmaltz (rendered chicken fat with onion), the by-product of the rendered fat is skin, out of which all the water and fat have been cooked, leaving mainly crispy protein, called gribenes, or chicken cracklings. Rillons (page 219) in a sense are like cracklings, given that the fat attached to the chunks of pork belly has been cooked and then crisped. Cracklings differ from Chicharrón (page 220) in a fundamental way: Chicharrón are cooked in water until they are tender and have rendered out most of their gelatin and fat. They are then scraped of any residual fat, leaving just the skin. Without all its encumbrances, the skin is free to puff when dropped into hot oil—to express its true nature, we like to think. Cracklings, on the other hand, are cooked only briefly, and the fat is retained (and helps cook them), so that when the skin crisps, you are left with a crispy, chewy, delicious protein-rich snack. Brian has concocted a simple seasoning for these addictive treats.

2 pounds pork rind from the shoulder or belly, cut into 1-by-¼-inch/2.5-by-0.5-centimeter strips

1½ teaspoons/8 grams kosher salt

1 tablespoon sweet or hot smoked paprika (preferably pimentón de la Vera)

1 teaspoon freshly ground black pepper

1 teaspoon garlic powder

½ teaspoon cayenne pepper

1. Preheat the oven to 400°F/205°C.

2. Bring a large pot of salted water to a boil. Add the rinds and cook for 20 to 30 minutes. They should be tender enough to pinch a hole in them with thumb and finger. Strain, rinse, cool, and pat dry. Season with the salt.

3. Line a rimmed baking sheet with parchment paper and spread the rinds out in a single layer. Roast, turning the rinds a couple of times to ensure even cooking, until crispy, 35 to 40 minutes. Transfer to paper towels to drain.

4. Toss the paprika, black pepper, garlic powder, and cayenne together and sprinkle the mixture evenly over the cracklings. Serve hot.

YIELD: 12 TO 15 APPETIZER PORTIONS

Braised Pork Belly with Five-Spice Powder

This is an excellent way to use pork belly, either as a featured item or as a component in another dish. Brian often uses the preparation as an accompaniment to another meat, which allows him to extend the more expensive protein while adding the complexities of varying flavors and textures—for example, by serving miso-glazed duck breast with a slab of crispy pork belly, broccoli rabe, and sticky purple rice. Here the belly is first braised to cook and tenderize it completely; it's then chilled, sliced, and sautéed as needed.

> 3 pounds/1.5 kilograms meaty pork belly, skin removed
>
> 6 tablespoons/90 grams kosher salt
>
> 2 tablespoons five-spice powder
>
> 1 tablespoon whole black peppercorns, toasted and ground
>
> 2 heads garlic, sliced horizontally in half
>
> ¼ cup/60 milliliters vegetable oil

1. Season the pork belly with the salt, five-spice powder, and pepper. Place it and the garlic in a large zip-top plastic bag or a covered, nonreactive container and refrigerate for at least 8 hours or up to 24 hours.

2. Preheat the oven to 325°F/160°C.

3. In an oven-safe sauté pan just large enough to contain the belly, heat the oil over medium-high heat. When the oil is hot, add the pork belly and cook until one side is nicely browned, 3 to 4 minutes. Flip the belly and sear the other side. Add enough water to come halfway up the sides of the pork belly. Bring the pan to a simmer, cover it, and put it in the oven until the belly is fork tender, about 3 hours.

4. Pour off the water (and reserve for another use if you wish—it will have a porky Asian flavor). When the pork and the pan are cool enough to handle, cover the pan with plastic wrap and weight the belly evenly (using another pan) to compress the fat and make the belly more uniform. Refrigerate until thoroughly chilled.

5. To serve, cut the belly in 1-inch/ 2.5-centimeter slices and sauté until heated through.

YIELD: 12 APPETIZER PORTIONS OR 8 PORTIONS TO COMPLEMENT A MAIN DISH

Chinese Crispy Pork Belly

This is similar to Rillons (page 219) in that the belly is crispy on the outside and tender and juicy on the inside. The technique is easy and yields a bubbly, crackling-type skin but tender, juicy meat and fat in the center, with the aromatic Asian spice blend that works so well with pork. This makes a lot and will last at least a week in the fridge.

Serve as a stand-alone appetizer or hors d'oeuvres (people can't resist it), or use it as a component in an Asian noodle dish like pho.

5 pounds/2.25 kilograms thick pork belly, skin on

Dry sherry as needed

1 tablespoon five-spice powder

Kosher salt as needed

1. With a sharp, pointy utensil, prick holes all over the pork belly skin (known as "docking")—the more the better for releasing liquid fat, but be careful not to go so deep into the fat below the skin that you pierce the flesh. Rub the belly well on all sides with dry sherry, then with the five-spice powder. Place in a large zip-top plastic bag or a covered, nonreactive container and refrigerate for at least 12 hours or up to 24 hours.

2. Preheat the oven to 350°F/175°C.

3. Lay a sheet of aluminum foil on the counter that is bigger than the belly. Put the belly in the center and fold the foil edges up to create a makeshift roasting pan so that the juices stay close to the belly. The foil should come up the sides of the belly so that only the skin is exposed. Place the foil pan with the pork belly in a roasting pan.

4. Cover the skin with a thick, even layer of kosher salt, enough to form a crust.

5. Roast the belly for 1 to 1½ hours, depending on the thickness, until it's fork tender. Turn on the broiler. Brush off the salt, then broil until the skin is crispy. Serve hot.

YIELD: 15 PORTIONS TO COMPLEMENT A MAIN DISH

Condiments

All pâtés, whether en croûte or en terrine, as a galantine or even a hot ballotine, benefit from a condiment or sauce.

Granted, some pâtés are so interesting, so rich in interior garnishes with varying flavors, colors, and textures, that you almost don't need a sauce. But generally, a pâté can be improved with a condiment or sauce, and rillettes can be enhanced with a really good mustard.

All dishes—everything we eat, really— are a combination of flavors and effects on the tongue (sweet, sour, salty, fatty, lean, umami, bitter), and often the dishes we like best are not necessarily those with the "best" flavor but those that possess the most interesting contrasts. That's why we find, say, Thai and Vietnamese food so interesting, because of the dramatic contrasts between sweet and sour and spicy, the sharp acidity of lime paired with salty-umami fish sauce. In our experience, cooks rarely go too far with the contrasts, but rather don't go far enough. When you're tasting, *try* to go too far with the acid and pull yourself back so you understand where the boundaries are.

Some condiments are so good they can make the dish (see the Dried Tart Cherry Marmalade, page 231). And given that many of the recipes in this book are meant to be served as a first course, you really want to captivate your audience from the get-go, so put a little effort into your sauces and condiments.

The following condiments fall into a variety of categories. Thick, chutney-like condiments, mustards, a vegetable puree, an all-purpose vinaigrette that can be thought of as a base, pickles, and one curio, the salt-cured egg yolk. The one category that's not common in the charcutier's kitchen is a mayonnaise-based condiment, because these preparations are so rich we don't need to pair them with a heavy, fat-based sauce, though a sweet-sour Sauce Gribiche (page 230) is rich but also goes well with pork. Vegetable and seafood terrines, which are relatively lean, can support such a condiment, like our Avocado and Herb Aioli (page 230).

It's important to have a mustard, a vinaigrette, mayonnaise, a chutney, and a pickle in your rotation; once you have a good grasp of the basics, you can vary them intuitively.

Whole-Grain Mustard

Mustard is one of the oldest condiments—it was used in ancient Rome and had probably been around for much longer. It was probably first made from mustard seeds ground with wine or must. The term *mustard* combines that word with a word for "hot" or "fiery," *ardent*. It's very easy to make your own, though it requires a week or two sitting in the fridge for the flavors to mellow, so plan ahead if you want to serve your own whole-grain mustard. It's a pleasure to make at a time when we think only of condiments that come in jars or plastic squeeze bottles. The three most common mustard seeds are yellow, which are the mildest, then brown and black, which pack more heat. Use a good craft pale ale here for the best flavor.

½ cup/78 grams yellow mustard seeds

½ cup/78 grams brown mustard seeds

½ cup/120 milliliters sherry wine vinegar

½ cup/120 milliliters craft pale ale or other beer

2 tablespoons light brown sugar

3 tablespoons honey

Kosher salt to taste

1. Combine the mustard seeds, vinegar, and beer in a bowl. Stir, cover, and let sit at room temperature until the liquid has been absorbed into the seeds, about 12 hours.

2. Transfer the seeds to a food processor, add the brown sugar, honey, and salt, and pulse five or six times to blend everything together.

3. Transfer the mustard to a clean container, cover, and refrigerate for 10 or 12 days before using; time will allow some of the harshness to mellow. The mustard will keep for several months in the refrigerator.

YIELD: ABOUT 2 CUPS/480 MILLILITERS

Horseradish-Beer Mustard

There are a number of ways to prepare mustard. Make your own using whole seeds (see page 228) or simply add water to Coleman's ground mustard for a nasal-clearing spread. We think of this as a pub mustard, or a cooked mustard. It is more like a sauce, with a flavorful liquid thickened with egg yolks and seasoned with mustard powder and fresh horseradish.

4 ounces/110 grams grated
fresh horseradish

¼ cup/65 grams light brown sugar

6 tablespoons/90 milliliters honey

6 large egg yolks

3 tablespoons Worcestershire sauce

3 tablespoons Coleman's ground mustard

1 cup/240 milliliters dark beer

1 cup/240 milliliters malt vinegar

Kosher salt to taste

1. Combine all the ingredients in the top of a double boiler and whisk together. Place over simmering water and whisk continuously until the mixture is thick.

2. Transfer the mustard to an airtight container and store in the refrigerator for up to 1 month.

YIELD: ABOUT 3 CUPS/720 MILLILITERS

Vinaigrette

This is a basic vinaigrette, flavored simply with shallot and mustard, that we intend to be a base for other ingredients that might make it specific to various pâtés. Add diced tomato and cucumber for the Shrimp, Scallop, and Saffron Terrine (page 89), or fresh tarragon for the Lobster Terrine (page 79), or diced dried fruit for any of the pork pâtés. Or add Garlic Confit (page 177) or Roasted Eggplant Caviar (page 236). It's infinitely variable. A standard vinaigrette is 3 parts oil to 1 part acid, but you can make it more acidic by changing that ratio to 2 to 1.

½ cup/120 milliliters vinegar (red wine, white wine, or champagne)

2 tablespoons Dijon mustard

1 tablespoon minced shallot

¼ teaspoon salt

Freshly ground black pepper to taste

1 to 1½ cups/240 to 360 milliliters vegetable oil and/or extra virgin olive oil

Combine the vinegar, mustard, shallot, salt, and pepper in a bowl and whisk well. Add the oil a few drops at a time while whisking, then add the remaining oil in a steady stream and whisk to emulsify. Refrigerate in an airtight container for up to 1 week.

YIELD: 1½ TO 2 CUPS/360 TO 480 MILLILITERS

Avocado and Herb Aioli

This fat-based sauce, further enriched with avocado and flavored with abundant herbs, is the perfect partner for a lean terrine, especially the Lobster Terrine (page 79) or Two-Potato Terrine (page 96). This will keep for a day or so, but it's best made at the time you want to use it.

    2 large egg yolks

    2 tablespoons fresh lemon juice

    1 teaspoon white wine vinegar

    1 garlic clove, lightly smashed

    ½ teaspoon/3 grams kosher salt

    1 ripe avocado, pitted and peeled

    ½ cup/30 grams chopped fresh
    soft herbs (such as basil, tarragon,
    chives, and/or flat-leaf parsley)

    2 cups/480 milliliters extra virgin olive oil

1. Combine the egg yolks, lemon juice, vinegar, garlic, and salt in a food processor and pulse to combine. Add the avocado and herbs and pulse until combined.

2. With the processor running, add the oil in a thin stream to create a thick sauce.

YIELD: ABOUT 2 CUPS/480 MILLILITERS

Sauce Gribiche

This sauce, a gussied-up tartar sauce, is traditionally served with pork and will go beautifully with just about any of the pâtés. We especially recommend it for the pig's head preparations. It is best served on the day it's made.

    3 large hard-cooked eggs

    1½ teaspoons Dijon mustard

    1 tablespoon fresh lemon juice

    2 teaspoons white wine vinegar

    Kosher salt to taste

    ¾ cup/180 milliliters vegetable oil

    1 tablespoon capers

    3 tablespoons chopped cornichons

    1 tablespoon minced fresh tarragon

    1 teaspoon minced fresh flat-leaf parsley

    Freshly ground black pepper to taste

1. Separate the egg yolks from the whites. Press the yolks through a fine-mesh sieve into a medium bowl. Add the mustard, lemon juice, and vinegar. Season with salt.

2. Whisking continuously, add the oil, drop by drop at first and then in a steady stream, until all the oil is incorporated in a thick emulsion.

3. Finely dice the egg whites and fold them into the sauce, along with the remaining ingredients. Taste and adjust the seasoning, adding more lemon juice and/or salt and pepper as necessary.

YIELD 1 CUP/240 MILLILITERS

Dried Tart Cherry Marmalade

This condiment was born out of Brian's Michigan heritage: tart cherries, one of the agricultural treasures of the Midwest. These bright red beauties, like other tart fruits and vegetables (rhubarb, Key limes), are beautifully suited not only to desserts but to condiments as well. Tart cherries, water, and a little sugar, so that the balance remains on the tart side, are all you really need. But Brian has put together a counterintuitive mixture of flavors, including honey, soy, garlic, and Tabasco, along with the crunch of almonds, to create a complex and beguiling condiment.

10 ounces/280 grams dried tart cherries

1½ cups/360 milliliters apple cider

½ cup/120 milliliters honey

2 tablespoons soy sauce

2 drops Tabasco

Grated zest and juice of 1 lemon

½ teaspoon minced garlic

4 ounces/110 grams sliced almonds, toasted

1. Combine all the ingredients except the almonds in a thick-bottomed, nonreactive pot with straight sides. Bring to a simmer slowly and cook until thick and syrupy, 20 to 30 minutes.

2. Remove the pan from the heat and allow it to cool, then fold in the almonds.

3. Store in an airtight container in the refrigerator for up to 3 weeks.

YIELD: ABOUT 2 CUPS/480 MILLILITERS

Onion Marmalade

This is a great make-ahead condiment to serve with just about any of the pâtés in this book or, really, anything fatty. It's an argument that supports Brian's belief that the onion should be thought of as a seasoning rather than a vegetable. While all onions will lose their harsh, acidic qualities to cooking and leave only sweetness, we still prefer naturally sweet onions such as Vidalia or Walla Walla (which are often less expensive than ordinary Spanish or yellow onions).

This preparation owes some of its jam-like consistency to pectin, a starch found in certain fruits that is used as a thickener. Pectin is usually found with the canning supplies at the grocery store.

2 tablespoons vegetable oil

1 pound/450 grams sweet onions, thinly sliced

Kosher salt and freshly ground black pepper to taste

2 cups/480 milliliters orange juice

½ cup/120 milliliters honey

Juice of 1 lemon

1½ teaspoons fresh thyme leaves

½ teaspoon pectin

1. Heat the oil in a large sauté pan over medium heat. Add the onions and sauté until they soften but before they begin to brown. Season them with salt and pepper. Add the orange juice and honey. Bring to a boil over high heat, then lower the heat so that the liquid simmers gently.

2. Add the lemon juice and thyme leaves and cook until the liquid has reduced to a few tablespoons.

3. Strain the liquid into a small dish. Sprinkle the pectin over the liquid and stir until it dissolves, then drizzle the liquid over the onions. Stir to ensure that the pectin is dissolved and evenly distributed.

4. Transfer the onions to a container, cover, and refrigerate until completely chilled and thickened. Store in the refrigerator for up to 1 month.

YIELD: 1½ CUPS/360 MILLILITERS

CLOCKWISE FROM TOP LEFT: Dried Tart Cherry Marmalade (page 231); Mango, Ginger, and Jalapeño Chutney (page 234); Onion Marmalade (page 232); Horseradish-Beer Mustard (page 229); Whole-Grain Mustard (page 228); Roasted Eggplant Caviar (page 236)

Mango, Ginger, and Jalapeño Chutney

This is a dynamic mixture worth having on hand, one of those condiments that can make a dish. It enlivens a pork pâté in a way that goes beyond mustard and pickles. There are a lot of ingredients, but they are simply combined in a pan and cooked until the chutney thickens.

3 mangos, pitted, peeled, and diced small (you should get about 1½ pounds/680 grams mango flesh)

3 ounces/85 grams golden raisins

2 ounces/60 grams minced jalapeño (seeds included if you like it spicy)

1 tablespoon minced garlic

1 tablespoon grated fresh ginger

1 cup/200 grams light brown sugar

1 cup/240 milliliters champagne vinegar

1 cinnamon stick

1 teaspoon ground turmeric

½ teaspoon/3 grams kosher salt

Pinch ground allspice

1. Combine all the ingredients in a thick-bottomed, nonreactive pan and bring to a simmer. Reduce the heat to low and cook until thick and syrupy, 20 to 30 minutes.

2. Store in an airtight container in the refrigerator for up to 1 month.

YIELD: ABOUT 3 CUPS/720 MILLILITERS

Pickled Ramps

When you're a cook raised in the Great Lakes region, the ramp is its own season. This wild leek begins to appear with the first breath of spring, so we associate it with light and hopefulness. Harvest them yourself or find them at farmers' markets.

Chefs are always looking for new ways to use ramps because they are so abundant in April and May. But here we use an old method, one that preserves the ramp so that we can make use of it in all its abundance. Once they're pickled, we can enjoy them throughout the summer and well into the fall. Pickled ramps make an outstanding condiment for just about every pâté, but especially those made with meat. (And if spring is late in your part of the world, this recipe works great with scallions.)

1 pound/450 grams ramps

¾ cup/180 milliliters water

½ cup/120 milliliters white wine vinegar

½ cup/130 grams sugar

1 tablespoon/15 grams kosher salt

1 teaspoon whole black peppercorns

1 teaspoon yellow mustard seeds

½ teaspoon cumin seeds

½ teaspoon caraway seeds

1 bay leaf

1. Wash the ramps and trim the green leaves to about 1 inch/2.5 centimeters up from the white part. (The green leaves are edible; mince them and add to scrambled eggs, or use in stock.) Trim the root end as you would a scallion.

2. Bring a pot of salted water to a rapid boil and prepare an ice bath. Add the ramps to the boiling water and blanch till just tender, a minute or two. Drain and shock in the ice bath. Pat the ramps dry and place in a heat-safe container that has a tight-fitting lid.

3. Combine the remaining ingredients in a saucepan and bring to a boil, stirring to dissolve the sugar. Cook for a few minutes, then pour the hot mixture over the ramps, cover, and cool to room temperature. Refrigerate for up to 3 weeks.

YIELD: 1 POUND/450 GRAMS

Roasted Eggplant Caviar

For this all-purpose condiment, we first char the eggplant over flames and then roast it to further develop the flavor. It works well as a sauce on pizza, a base for a canapé or crostini, or a dip with crackers or crusty bread, or it can be added to Vinaigrette (page 229) to lend an earthy flavor to salads.

2 large eggplants (about 3 pounds/
1.5 kilograms total)

½ cup/120 milliliters extra virgin olive oil

½ cup/70 grams minced onion

1 cup/240 milliliters peeled, seeded,
and chopped plum tomatoes

2 tablespoons minced garlic

1 tablespoon fresh lemon juice

Kosher salt and freshly ground
black pepper to taste

1. Preheat the oven to 350°F/175°C.

2. On a gas grill or open flame on a stove, char the skin of the eggplants all over.

3. Use 1 tablespoon of the olive oil to grease a rimmed baking sheet. Place the eggplants on the sheet and roast until very soft, 30 or 40 minutes. When the eggplants are cool enough to handle, peel and seed them.

4. Place the eggplant pulp in the bowl of a food processor and add the remaining ingredients. Puree until smooth, a minute or so. This will keep for a week in the refrigerator.

YIELD: ABOUT 3 CUPS/720 MILLILITERS

Salt-Cured Egg Yolks

This is just plain fun, to transform the common egg yolk from a fluid encased in a fine membrane into a solid using salt rather than heat. Once cured, these yolks can be grated over just about anything for added color and flavor—pasta, salads, soups, even hard cheeses. And they're especially good grated over any of the seafood pâtés and rillettes. You can cure the egg yolks with salt alone, you can mellow the salt by mixing in a half part sugar, or, as we do here, you can add spicy seasonings to the salt to impart to the yolks.

Note that you must remove the chalazae, the white cords that keep the yolk suspended in the albumen, or the yolks may not solidify. Try to use the freshest eggs possible—the vitelline membrane surrounding the yolk must be intact, of course, and will be sturdier in fresher eggs.

1½ pounds/680 grams kosher salt

6 tablespoons/40 grams freshly ground black pepper

2 tablespoons red pepper flakes

Leaves from 1 bunch fresh thyme

10 large egg yolks

1. In a bowl, combine the salt, black pepper, red pepper flakes, and thyme leaves. Pour a layer of the mixture about ¾ inch/2 centimeters deep into a 12-by-6-inch/30-by-15-centimeter pan or baking dish, or any nonreactive container that will hold the yolks, such as a pie plate. Make 10 indentations in the salt layer.

2. Carefully crack each egg and place one yolk in each indentation. (Reserve the whites for another use.) Carefully cover the yolks with the remaining salt mixture. Cover and refrigerate for 5 days.

3. Remove the yolks from the salt, brush off the excess, and store in an airtight container in the refrigerator for up to 1 month.

YIELD: 10 CURED YOLKS

ACKNOWLEDGMENTS

I teach about 120 students a year. Some are the same kind of knucklehead I was when I started cooking. Others arrive with the kind of knowledge I had to work years to get. None of them deserve me. (Kidding.)

Few of them, if any, knew they were helping me work on this book. (Not kidding.)

They tested these recipes as they learned the craft of charcuterie. I am grateful to each one of them, especially for what they teach me.

I'm very lucky to work at Schoolcraft College outside Detroit, where I've been teaching since 1997, even while I was the chef-owner of half a dozen restaurants in my home state of Michigan. Shawn Loving was uncommonly supportive and inspirational in his own quest to be the best a chef can be. Jeff Gabriel insisted his bread be featured somewhere because what is fatty food without bread (pages 66 and 208). Joe Decker, who has been a lifelong friend (even though he's a pastry chef), contributed the finest pâté en croûte dough to this book. I urge anyone who makes a pâté en croûte to use that Decker Dough (page 141); it should be a regular part of your repertoire. Sous chef Jake Draves, the badass cage fighter who kept me organized and in line. All of them are extraordinary chefs I'm lucky to work beside.

Finally, I want to thank Milos Cihelka, my mentor, who introduced me to forcemeats and pâtés in 1980, showing me the way a chef could take underutilized cuts of meat and trim and turn them into delicious food that looks beautiful and lasts longer (and makes money!). In this way, the forcemeat is really the heart and soul of any professional kitchen and truly great chef.

Last thanks to my wife, Julia, and to each of my five kids, Alana, Alex, Carmen, Dylan, and Ben.

—Brian Polcyn

I'd like to thank Chef Brian, who conceived and drove the book forward. I learned more in writing it than I thought possible. Brian and I would both like to thank the team at Norton: Melanie Tortoroli, Nathaniel Dennett, Anna Oler, Susan Sanfrey, Ingsu Liu, and the many people who helped make this book a reality: Karen Wise, Toni Tajima, Joe Vaughn, Elizabeth Parson, and so many others.

We'd also like to thank all those who take the time to read this book, to cook from it, to make a pâté. You are the ones keeping this craft a vibrant part of the American kitchen.

—Michael Ruhlman

INDEX

Note: Page references in *italics* indicate photographs.